Finding Peace When Your Heart Is in Pieces

Break Free from Emotional Pain and Feel Whole Again—A Soulful Guide to Healing After Loss, Heartbreak, or Trauma

by

Yasmin Zeller

information does not mean that the author or the publisher endorses the information the organization or website may provide or recommendations it may make.

Please remember that Internet websites listed in this work may have changed or disappeared between when this work was written and when it is read.

Finding Peace When Your Heart Is in
Pieces : Break Free from Emotional Pain
and Feel Whole Again—A Soulful Guide to
Healing After Loss, Heartbreak, or Trauma

TABLE OF CONTENTS

INTRODUCTION

Heartbreak, loss, and betrayal. These are experiences that leave us feeling exposed, vulnerable, and often, utterly shattered. When someone you love walks away or a sudden loss shakes your world, it's as if the ground beneath your feet gives way. You find yourself navigating an emotional landscape that feels foreign and overwhelming. It is in these moments that peace seems almost impossible to grasp. Yet, even in the depths of such pain, there is a path forward. This book aims to be a companion on that journey—the quiet, steady hand guiding you through the storm toward healing and renewal.

The heart's fractures may feel like they mark an ending, but they also signify a beginning. So often, people carry their brokenness in silence, believing that the cracks make them less whole. But the truth is quite the opposite. It's through acknowledging the pain and facing it head-on that transformation becomes possible. Finding peace when your heart is in pieces isn't about forgetting what happened or rushing past your emotions; it's about tending to those wounds with care, honesty, and patience. It is an act of courage to show up, sit with your pain, and slowly piece yourself back together.

Everyone's pain looks different. For some, it's the lingering ache left behind by a relationship that once felt like home. For others, it's the sudden void created by a loss that no one could prepare them for. Betrayal cuts in ways that feel personal and devastating. But whatever form your heartbreak takes, this book invites you to step into a space where those feelings are valid and where healing starts by simply allowing yourself to feel what's real. There's no timeline that fits everyone; no instruction manual on how you "should" grieve. Instead, what you'll find here is comfort, understanding, and a roadmap tailored to your own pace.

One of the hardest things about emotional trauma is how isolating it can feel. It's easy to believe that you're alone in your suffering or that no one else truly understands what you're going through. When the world seems distant and your heart heavy, you might wonder if you'll ever experience happiness again. This introduction acknowledges that truth head-on— that the journey through deep emotional pain is raw and messy. But it also holds a powerful, unwavering hope: that healing is possible, and peace does await beyond the sorrow.

This guide is written with empathy and intent. Recognizing your courage for seeking healing is the first step. There is strength in your willingness to face brokenness rather than avoid it. You aren't defined by your losses or the moments you wished had been different. Instead, you can reclaim your story and discover parts of yourself you might have never seen before. Your pain contains the seed of growth, even if it doesn't feel that way now.

In the pages that follow, you'll find not only guidance but also reassurance that it's okay to feel overwhelmed or uncertain. Healing isn't a linear path, nor is it a matter of simply "getting over it." It involves embracing vulnerability, allowing yourself to experience grief fully, and then choosing to take compassionate steps forward. The goal here is to help you build a foundation rooted in understanding and self-compassion, providing tools to gradually rebuild and rediscover your inner peace.

When your heart is broken, the whole body feels it— the tension in your shoulders, the fluttering in your stomach, the weight that settles in your chest. Emotional pain isn't just a matter of thought or feeling; it influences how you move through the world each day. That's why healing needs to engage all parts of you: mind, body, and spirit. This book nurtures that holistic approach, offering insights and practices that can support restorative growth on every level.

Whether this heartbreak happened yesterday or years ago, whether your wounds are fresh or have been hidden beneath the surface, there's a place for you here. This isn't about rushing toward a happy ending or pretending the pain doesn't exist. It's about honoring your experience exactly as it is and creating room for a future where peace feels authentic and within reach. You hold more power than you realize to shape your healing.

And just as important, this book is rooted in the reality that healing can only happen when you allow yourself the grace to be imperfect. You won't have all the answers, and your feelings may shift from moment to moment. This is expected, normal, and part of the human experience. By adopting a gentle and encouraging mindset, you can create the inner space necessary to move through darkness into the light of renewal.

Keep in mind that peace does not mean forgetting or becoming immune to pain. It means learning to live alongside your story with greater ease, acceptance, and resilience. Your heartbreak has shaped you, but it will not define you. There are new chapters waiting, filled with hope, growth, and meaningful connections. You are invited to lean into this process with curiosity and openness, stepping forward one day at a time.

This introduction sets the tone for the chapters ahead, which explore the nature of pain, the inward journey of emotional recovery, and practical ways to rebuild your life. But here, it's simply the acknowledgment that to be broken is human—and to heal is profoundly transformative. You are not alone in this experience. Many have walked this path from darkness toward peace and emerged stronger and more whole. This book is your invitation to do the same.

Take a deep breath and let yourself arrive here fully, with all the questions, fears, and hopes you carry. There is no rush. Healing unfolds in its own time, and this is your sacred space to discover what that looks like for you. May you find comfort in these words and strength in your own beautiful resilience.

CHAPTER I

UNDERSTANDING THE PAIN

When your heart shatters from loss, betrayal, or the end of something deeply cherished, it feels like the world has stopped making sense. This kind of pain isn't just emotional—it winds through your mind, body, and spirit, leaving invisible wounds that others might not see but that you live with every day. Understanding the rawness of your suffering is the first step toward healing, even though it often feels overwhelming and endless. Healing doesn't mean forgetting or "getting over it" as some might suggest; it means facing the truth of your pain, recognizing how profoundly it's shaped your experience, and gently beginning to make room for hope. It's important to acknowledge that healing is never linear nor quick—it's messy, complicated, and deeply personal. What you're going through is real, and this journey requires patience, kindness to yourself, and the courage to stay present with all the feelings that come up. This is not about rushing past the pain but learning to live with it until one day, it softens enough to let peace bloom in its place.

When Life Breaks You Open

There's a moment—often sudden, sometimes slow—when life shatters the illusion of control we cling to. This breaking open isn't just a metaphor; it's the raw, exposed reality of emotional pain demanding your full attention. When life breaks you open, it exposes parts of yourself you've either kept hidden or never fully understood. The ache that follows a breakup, betrayal, or loss rends through your heart and soul, leaving you feeling vulnerable, disoriented, and often, utterly alone. Yet, paradoxically, this breaking open is the doorway to deeper healing and transformation.

It's important to recognize that this rupture in your emotional armor isn't a sign of weakness or failure. It's a profoundly human experience signaling that something significant has shifted in your life. When the familiar structure dissolves—whether that's a relationship, a trusted friendship, or a dream you held dear—it leaves behind a cavernous space inside you. That space may feel like a vacuum at first, and it can be terrifying to face. But it also invites you to rediscover who you are beneath the pain, beneath the loss.

At times, the breaking open can feel relentless, like a storm battering your soul with wave after wave of grief and confusion. This intensity is disorienting, and your mind may scramble to make sense of what's happening. You might find yourself replaying moments, wondering what could have been different, or trying to grasp at some control over an uncontrollable situation. It's normal to resist this process; after all, no one wants to be stripped of their stability and certainty. But resistance often prolongs suffering. The more you allow yourself to be present even to the most unbearable emotions, the more you create room for healing to begin.

Imagine, for a moment, that the breaking open is like a seed cracking through the soil. Beneath the surface, something new is ready to grow—something that couldn't have blossomed without that initial breaking. This doesn't mean you're expected to leap happily beyond your pain or quickly "move on." Instead, the fracture invites you into a deeper relationship with yourself. It calls you to feel your feelings honestly, to lean into your vulnerability without judgment, and to recognize your capacity for resilience and renewal.

The process of being broken open sheds light on hidden wounds you might have carried silently for years. These wounds are often not visible to the outside world, but they shape how you view yourself and your ability to trust again. Beneath the immediate hurt, there might be old fears of abandonment, self-doubt, or an aching loneliness. When life breaks you open, it pulls these layers to the surface, sometimes unexpectedly. Though painful, this exposure offers a chance to confront these wounds rather than bury them deeper.

It's essential to honor this breaking open as a sacred, albeit painful, rite of passage. It can feel impossible to imagine peace in the midst of such rawness, but the paradox is that through embracing the pain rather than fleeing from it, you slowly reclaim your power. The breaking open dismantles the protective walls you built, but in doing so, it also makes way for authentic connection—with yourself and others. This renewed connection is the foundation of true healing.

One of the hardest truths to accept in this space is that healing doesn't follow a neat, linear path. When you're broken open, your emotions might swing wildly from numbness to despair, from anger to moments of fragile hope. This unpredictability can feel discouraging, but it's a sign that your inner world is shifting. There's no timeline for when the storm will pass or how it will reshape you. The only commitment that matters is to stay with yourself through it all.

During this time, self-compassion becomes your greatest ally. Instead of judging yourself for feeling vulnerable, scared, or overwhelmed, extend kindness inward. When life breaks you open, you deserve patience—not only from others but especially from yourself. The voice inside that criticizes or urges you to "get over it" isn't grounded in your best interest. Instead, listen to the small, gentle parts of you that whisper words of comfort.

It's also helpful to remember that being broken open doesn't mean you have to face everything alone. Though it may feel isolating, reaching out for support can provide much-needed relief. Sometimes a conversation with a trusted friend, a therapist, or a support group can remind you that your pain is valid and that others have walked similar paths. Transparent, compassionate connection is a powerful antidote to the loneliness this pain often breeds.

In the silence after the breaking, you might discover unexpected strengths. Pain has a strange way of teaching endurance, patience, and a deeper empathy for others. You may start to see your story in a new light—not just as one of loss, but as part of a larger narrative of growth and awakening. The cracks in your heart become places where light can enter in, illuminating parts of your soul that remained in shadow before.

When life breaks you open, it demands that you reimagine what peace means for you. Peace isn't the absence of pain or struggle. Instead, it's more like a quiet center within the chaos—a place where you can sit with your whole experience without needing to fix or escape it. Cultivating this kind of peace takes courage because it means inviting discomfort instead of resisting it. Yet in this courageous invitation, healing begins to take root.

The breaking open also challenges you to examine old stories you've told yourself about who you are, what you deserve, and what love looks like. These stories may have consoled you once, but they can become barriers when they no longer serve your healing. Pain uncovers these narratives and offers a chance to rewrite them with more truth and compassion. Over time, what was shattered makes way for a more authentic and empowered sense of self.

Remember, this experience is not a sign you're broken beyond repair. It's evidence that your spirit is alive and demanding attention. The cracks are not failures; they're invitations to rediscover your capacity for hope, for love, and for joy—even when your heart feels in pieces. Life breaking you open is a difficult but profound turning point that can lead to a richer, fuller engagement with yourself and the world.

So, as you sit with this section of your journey, know that the pain isn't the end. It's the opening chapter of your new story. Healing is not about erasing the breaking, but rather weaving it into the fabric of who you become—a person deeply human, resilient, and beautifully alive in every imperfect way.

Recognizing Loss, Heartbreak, and Emotional Trauma

Loss is one of the most profound experiences we face in life, often arriving without warning and shaking the very foundation of our emotional world. Whether it's the end of a relationship, the death of a loved one, or a deep betrayal, these moments leave a mark that feels both heavy and overwhelming. It's important to recognize that loss isn't just about an event; it's about the way that event fractures our inner reality. When the familiar is suddenly gone, it creates a rupture that takes time and care to mend.

Heartbreak, in all its forms, isn't always visible to the outside world. Unlike physical wounds, emotional injuries don't have a cast or a scar that others can see. Instead, they manifest quietly in the crevices of our daily lives—through restless nights, an aching chest, or a numbness that seeps into even joyful moments. This pain can feel isolating. Many find themselves wondering if they're the only one suffering this deeply, if anyone else has been through this kind of heartbreak and survived intact.

Emotional trauma tied to loss and heartbreak often goes unrecognized, even by those experiencing it. We're conditioned to expect grief to follow a certain script: maybe a week of crying, some support from friends, and then a return to normal life. But trauma isn't linear. Its effects are messy, unpredictable, and sometimes chronic. Recognizing that what you're feeling is a legitimate emotional trauma is the first step toward healing. It validates your pain and reminds you that what you're going through is significant — worthy of attention and empathy.

It's natural to want to push away the pain or distract yourself from it. After all, pain can feel unbearable and all-consuming. Yet, every time you suppress or deny these feelings, they press harder against the fragile seams of your emotional being. Recognizing loss and heartbreak means giving yourself permission to acknowledge this pain without judgment. It means admitting that the heartbreak has changed you—that the person you were before isn't quite the person you are now, and that's okay.

Often, the roots of emotional trauma run deeper than the heartache itself. There may be layers of unresolved feelings, old wounds, or lingering insecurities that resurface when loss strikes. These wounds might have been dormant, hidden beneath everyday routines, until the loss cracked the foundation. Accepting this complexity is part of recognizing trauma. It's not about ignoring or simplifying the pain, but about honoring the full range of your emotional experience, however complicated it may be.

Loss doesn't discriminate. It doesn't matter if it's a romantic breakup, the betrayal of a close friend, or the death of a family member. The heart reacts with similar ferocity. That storm of emotions—sadness, anger, guilt, confusion—swirls within you. Sometimes it feels like drowning; at other times, it's more like being paralyzed, unable to move forward or backward. Recognizing this emotional upheaval as trauma, not just sadness or disappointment, helps to frame your journey differently.

Trauma has a way of distorting your sense of safety in the world. Where once you felt secure, connected, or hopeful, now you might experience fear, mistrust, or profound loneliness. You might find yourself withdrawing from people, not because you don't love them or want their company, but because everything feels like it could shatter at any moment. This hypersensitivity isn't a flaw—it's a natural response to having your emotional foundation shaken.

The intensity of heartbreak often leads to searching for answers: why did this happen? Was there something I could've done differently? These questions can spiral into self-blame or regret, which only deepen the trauma. Recognizing emotional trauma means understanding that some things are out of your control. It also means learning to hold space for your grief without trying to rush the process with premature solutions or pressure to "move on." Your feelings are an essential part of your healing, not something to be hurried past.

It's also important to recognize how loss and heartbreak change the stories we tell ourselves. Your narrative before the loss might have been about trust, security, and predictability. But after trauma, that narrative often feels shattered or incomplete. This shift in self-perception can be disorienting. Recognizing it is crucial because it opens the door to rewriting your story—not by erasing the pain but by integrating it as part of your ongoing life chapter.

Sometimes, the hardest part is giving voice to what's been lost—that sense of belonging, identity, or hope that walked away with the person or situation that caused your heartbreak. When you begin to name what you've lost, it brings clarity and gentle acceptance. Naming helps to fight the invisibility of emotional trauma, making the unseen wounds visible to yourself and, when you're ready, to others. This brings connection, which is vital because healing rarely happens in isolation.

Recognizing the impact of loss on not just your mind but your body and spirit is another key part of this process. Emotional pain often triggers physical symptoms—tightness in the chest, fatigue, changes in appetite, or even chronic aches. You may feel disconnected from your spiritual core or lose faith in the flow of life, questioning everything you once held sacred. Seeing these reactions as part of trauma validates the whole person, not just the mind or emotions.

Loss, heartbreak, and emotional trauma aren't just moments in time—they're experiences that ripple through your entire being. Sometimes, the pain will catch you off guard, triggered by a song, a place, or a familiar scent. These moments remind you that healing is not about forgetting but about learning to live with the echoes of loss while finding your way back to peace.

Recognizing loss and heartbreak as trauma also helps to dismantle the stigma around emotional pain. Society often pressures us to "get over it" quickly, to appear strong and unshaken. But true strength lies in vulnerability—acknowledging your pain, giving it room to breathe, and reaching out when you need help. Trauma recognition is the doorway to this strength, the foundation on which you can rebuild your trust in yourself and others.

In this recognition, there's also hope. It signals the start of a transformative journey. By honoring your pain and trauma, you open the possibility of growth—not because the loss was necessary, but because your response to it can deepen your capacity for empathy, self-awareness, and resilience. Your heartbreak is not the end of your story, but the beginning of a new chapter, one that holds the power for healing and renewal.

The Invisible Wounds We Carry

When we experience emotional trauma—like heartbreak, loss, or betrayal—the scars we bear are often invisible. Unlike a broken bone, these wounds aren't visible to the eye. They don't show up on an X-ray or leave a physical mark we can point to. Yet, their pain can cut just as deep, shaping our inner world in silent, persistent ways. These invisible wounds live beneath the surface, tucked away in our thoughts, memories, and deepest feelings.

Carrying these wounds is like walking through life with a weight no one else can see. It's exhausting and isolating. You might find yourself struggling with a heaviness that's hard to explain. Maybe you push people away because you feel misunderstood, or you put on a brave face while inside, everything feels fragile and raw. What makes these wounds so tricky is that they demand healing, but healing isn't a straightforward process. The hurt lingers because it's tied to part of our identity, our relationships, and sometimes even our sense of safety and trust.

The very nature of emotional pain means we often hide it even from ourselves. Sometimes, we bury it so deep, we don't realize how much it affects us—how it clouds our judgment, sabotages our sense of self-worth, or keeps us stuck in patterns of fear and shame. Invisible wounds carry with them stories we haven't fully processed, feelings we've stuffed away, and longing for answers that may never come. This silence around our pain makes it feel even heavier, as though we're carrying it alone.

Our culture plays a huge role in how we experience these wounds. There's often an unspoken rule that emotional pain should be endured quietly or "gotten over" quickly. In the rush to appear okay, many suffer in silence, ashamed of showing vulnerability or asking for help. But in reality, healing demands courage—the courage to face what's hidden beneath the surface, to acknowledge those wounds without judgment, and to start the slow work of making peace with them.

These invisible wounds aren't just emotional. They live in our physical bodies too. You may have noticed how heartbreak can feel like a literal ache in your chest or how anxiety sometimes tightens your throat or knots your stomach. Trauma and unresolved grief trigger physical responses because the mind and body aren't separate. They're deeply connected. Emotional pain can cause sleepless nights, fatigue, headaches, and even digestive issues. What's happening inside reverberates outside, a constant reminder that healing requires tending to the whole self.

One of the hardest parts about invisible wounds is their unpredictability. A certain smell, a song, or a passing glance can reopen old pain without warning. These triggers often catch us off guard, pulling us back into moments we thought were behind us. That's because emotional trauma doesn't vanish with time alone; it's woven into the fabric of our memories and reactions. A wound like this isn't a simple cut you can bandage and forget. It's more like a scar that can sting on cold days, reminding you it's still there beneath the surface.

Another layer to these wounds is how they shape our relationships. When we're hurt deeply, especially by someone we trusted, it can alter how safe it feels to love or be loved. We might build walls around our hearts as a form of protection, but those walls can also isolate us. Feeling hurt and vulnerable makes it tempting to avoid intimacy altogether. Trust, which once may have come easily, becomes something scarce and precious. That's why healing invisible wounds often requires relearning how to connect, starting gently with ourselves and extending outwards when ready.

It's important to remember that carrying these wounds does not mean we are weak or broken beyond repair. In fact, the very act of surviving emotional trauma demands a kind of quiet bravery that isn't always visible on the outside. Each day you continue moving forward—even when it hurts—is an act of resilience. These wounds, while painful, also hold the potential for profound transformation. They invite us to step into deeper self-awareness, to uncover strength we never knew we had, and to rewrite the stories we tell ourselves about who we are and what we deserve.

Sometimes, the struggle with invisible wounds leaves us questioning our own reality. Did that hurt really happen? Am I overreacting? Such self-doubt is common because these wounds live in the realm of feelings and memories—not concrete proof. It's essential to recognize that our pain is valid, even if others don't see it or understand it. Trusting your own experience becomes a vital step in healing. When you begin to acknowledge your wounds with kindness and without minimizing them, you start reclaiming your power.

The journey with invisible wounds is rarely linear. There will be days when the pain feels raw and overwhelming, and others when it seems distant and manageable. Healing doesn't mean forgetting or erasing the wound altogether. Instead, it means learning to live with it differently; bringing those hidden parts of yourself into the light where they can be held, understood, and gently nurtured. This takes patience and, often, the support of others who can witness your story without judgment.

What transforms an invisible wound from a source of pain into a place of growth is the shift in how we relate to it. Instead of seeing the wound as a burden or a black mark on our worth, we can begin to view it as a chapter in our story—not the whole book. It's part of the landscape of our lives that has shaped us, but it does not define us. This perspective opens the door to compassion—both for ourselves and for those who may have unintentionally caused our pain.

Healing invisible wounds often starts with something deceptively small: giving yourself permission to acknowledge your pain without rushing to fix it. Feel it. Sit with it. Let it speak. This is the opposite of turning away; it's leaning in with an open heart. By doing so, you create space where healing can begin. You send a message to yourself that your feelings matter, that your experience is worthy of care.

From here, the path unfolds uniquely for each person. Some find solace in writing their pain down, others in talking to trusted friends or professionals. Meditation, art, movement, or simply spending quiet time in nature can help bring clarity and calm. What matters most is creating rituals of attention and compassion toward those hidden places inside. This kind of care helps the scar tissue soften and the hurt transform from something frozen into something fluid—something that moves and changes as you do.

Invisible wounds teach us that healing is a courage-rooted act of ongoing self-discovery. It means embracing vulnerability and uncertainty, but also meeting ourselves with the deepest kindness. In this tender unfolding, peace is not about forgetting pain but integrating it. Through this integration, there is an opportunity to emerge wiser, softer, and more open to love, even when our hearts have been broken into pieces.

How Emotional Pain Affects the Mind, Body, and Spirit

Emotional pain doesn't just hurt in our hearts—it reaches far deeper, intertwining with every part of who we are. When you're grappling with heartbreak, loss, or betrayal, the suffering seeps into your mind, your body, and your spirit, often in ways that can feel invisible or confusing. It's not just sadness; it's a force that can cloud your thoughts, weigh on your muscles, and hollow out your very sense of self. Understanding how these layers of pain connect is the first step toward finding peace.

Our minds are profoundly affected by emotional trauma. In the aftermath of losing someone we love or experiencing a deep wound in trust, thoughts can spiral into a relentless loop of doubt, anger, or self-questioning. You might find yourself replaying moments over and over, trying to puzzle out "what ifs" or "whys" that don't have answers. This mental exhaustion can lead to difficulty concentrating, decision fatigue, or even a kind of fog that clouds judgment and creativity.

It's important to recognize that these mental reactions aren't a sign of weakness or failure—they're natural responses to an intense emotional upheaval. Your brain is trying to make sense of the chaos. Sometimes, it overcompensates by fixating on painful memories or overanalyzing every detail as a way to regain control. When your mind is caught in this cycle, it can feel like you're trapped inside your own head, disconnected from the present moment and stuck in the pain of what's passed.

At the same time, emotional pain finds a direct path to the body. You've likely experienced this yourself—maybe as a tightness in your chest, a heaviness in your limbs, or a knotted stomach. It's the kind of ache that can't be explained by a simple physical injury but feels undeniably real. Stress hormones surge, your nervous system goes into high alert, and muscles tense without your conscious awareness. This chronic tension can lead to headaches, digestive issues, and even a lowered immune response, making it harder to recover physically and emotionally.

There's a reason people sometimes describe heartbreak as "brokenhearted" or say it "hurts in your gut"—emotional pain literally impacts your physiology. Your body remembers what your heart feels. This connection means that healing emotional wounds isn't just about changing your thoughts or feelings, but also about caring for the physical symptoms that arise. Rest, nourishment, gentle movement, and moments of stillness become essential tools to quiet your body's alarm bells.

Beyond mind and body, emotional pain touches something even more elusive: the spirit. This is the core of your being, the part that feels connected to meaning, purpose, and a sense of belonging in the world. When you're wounded emotionally, your spirit often feels fractured or adrift. You might question your place in life or wrestle with a loss of faith—not necessarily in the religious sense, but in the fundamental trust that life can be good, that you will be okay again.

This spiritual pain can leave you feeling empty, disconnected, or numb. It's as if a vital spark has dimmed or gone out altogether. But acknowledging this spiritual disruption is crucial because it reveals how deep the impact of emotional trauma really goes. Healing, then, isn't merely about fixing what's on the surface—it's about gently nurturing that inner flame back to life. Practices that foster connection—whether through meditation, nature, creative expression, or community—can serve as lifelines when the spirit feels lost.

Many people underestimate how intertwined these three elements—mind, body, and spirit—are when it comes to emotional suffering. Trying to heal by focusing on only one aspect may leave you feeling stuck or incomplete. For example, pushing yourself to "think positive" when your body is still tense or your spirit is shattered rarely brings lasting relief. Instead, healing happens in the spaces where we allow each part of ourselves to be seen, held, and understood.

The chaos of emotional pain also distorts our sense of time and reality. The mind, overwhelmed with grief or betrayal, can feel like it's caught in an endless loop of suffering. Physically, the body feels fatigued and depleted, yet restless or anxious at the same time. Spiritually, you might feel disconnected from the rhythms and meaning that once sustained you. This dissonance creates a powerful tension—one that can make even simple tasks seem monumental.

Recognizing how pain manifests across these dimensions invites compassion toward yourself. You're not simply "overthinking" or "overreacting." There's a very real impact here. Your mind, body, and spirit are responding to trauma in the only ways they know how. When you approach these symptoms with kindness rather than judgment, you open the door to true healing.

Healing also requires patience. The mind needs time to stop racing and begin to rest. The body needs space to relax and rebuild energy. The spirit needs room to rediscover its connection to life's bigger picture. Each part moves at its own pace, sometimes unevenly, but always toward greater wholeness. Try to cultivate grace for each step, knowing that pain is not a flaw but a sign that something precious was lost and needs careful mending.

In moments of despair, it can feel as if this pain will last forever. The mind may insist it won't get better, the body feels worn down beyond repair, and the spirit might whisper that you're alone in this struggle. But these feelings, as intense as they are, do not tell the whole story. We are resilient beings, designed not only to survive but to heal and grow. The intersection of mind, body, and spirit is where transformation happens—where brokenness can turn into wisdom, and sorrow can give rise to new hope.

You don't have to battle this pain in isolation. Every breath you take is a chance to bring gentle awareness to how your mind, body, and spirit are interacting. When you recognize the signs—tension in your muscles, racing thoughts, or a heaviness in your chest—you can begin to respond with intention instead of resistance. This might mean setting boundaries, practicing grounding exercises, or seeking out supportive relationships and communities that remind you that you are not alone.

Ultimately, the way emotional pain touches mind, body, and spirit is a profound invitation. It calls you to slow down, listen deeply to yourself, and care for your whole being in an integrated way. You may never "forget" the heartbreak, but you can learn to live differently with it—not as a broken person, but as one who has discovered an unshakeable source of strength and peace inside.

Why Healing Feels So Hard

Healing isn't a straight path, nor is it a quick fix. When your heart is shattered, the journey to wholeness can feel like wading through a vast, heavy fog where every step forward is met with resistance. This struggle is not a sign that you're weak or doing something wrong. It's simply the reality of how deeply we're wired to protect ourselves from pain, even when that protection slows down our recovery. The difficulty in healing stems from the tangled web of emotions, memories, and physical sensations, all colliding inside you and demanding attention at once.

One reason healing feels so hard is because emotional pain isn't just stored in the mind—it lives in the body. When we experience heartbreak, loss, or betrayal, our nervous system goes on high alert, triggering fight, flight, or freeze responses that evolved to keep us safe from immediate danger. But unlike escaping a physical threat, the wounds we carry from emotional trauma don't just vanish once the danger passes. Instead, they linger, holding us hostage to anxiety, mistrust, and even chronic stress. This ongoing tension can leave you feeling exhausted, mentally foggy, or physically unwell, making it that much harder to find the mental clarity and emotional space needed to heal.

The complexity of healing also comes from its unpredictable timeline. We often expect that grief or heartbreak will follow a neat, linear path—some period of sadness followed by gradual improvement—but real healing rarely works that way. Instead, it moves in spirals and waves, sometimes washing over you in unexpected outbursts or long, silent stretches of numbness. These ups and downs can create a sense of failure or frustration, as if you should be "over it" by now. In reality, this back-and-forth is normal and necessary. It's how your mind and body process what happened, test the waters of new emotional territory, and integrate fresh understanding of yourself and your experience.

Another part of this challenge lies in our often complicated relationship with emotional pain itself. Society tends to send a clear message: pain is something to avoid, suppress, or quickly overcome. We are told to "move on," "get over it," or "be strong." These phrases, while well-meaning, can actually make healing feel more isolating. When you're struggling with raw feelings, hearing others minimize your experience—or worse, questioning the legitimacy of your pain—only deepens your sense of loneliness. It's hard to give yourself permission to feel vulnerable when the world around you seems to demand resilience without cracks.

This outside pressure intersects with the internal voices that can be even harsher. Self-judgment and blame often sneak into the healing process, like an uninvited guest. You might ask yourself why you didn't see the signs sooner, wonder what you could have done differently, or criticize yourself for still feeling hurt. These thoughts take up mental space that could otherwise be used for self-compassion. They create a loop that traps you in guilt and shame, making it feel nearly impossible to break free and move forward.

What makes healing so elusive also has to do with how our brains are wired to handle trauma and loss. Emotional wounds tend to create what some researchers call "emotional memory networks." These are clusters of stored feelings, images, and sensations that can be triggered effortlessly by something as simple as a song, a smell, or a familiar phrase. When triggered, they pull you back into the pain as if it were happening all over again. This neurobiological response means that the past doesn't always stay in the past—it can live right alongside your present moment, sometimes without warning. Each time this happens, it feels like starting over, even if you've made progress before.

In addition to these neurological layers, healing feels hard because breaking down old attachments is inherently painful. Trauma, loss, and heartbreak are all about losing something meaningful—whether it's a person, a dream, or a sense of security. Letting go means stepping into the unknown, and as naturally human beings, we crave stability and certainty. Holding onto hurt—even when it brings suffering—can feel safer than risking further disappointment or betrayal. The mind creates stories to protect you from this fear, sometimes convincing you that the pain you have is better than the uncertainty ahead. So, the part of you that's trying to heal might also be fighting fiercely to hold onto what's familiar.

Another layer complicating healing is the often unspoken grief around the "what could have been." This is not just mourning what was lost but also the future you imagined with it. When a relationship ends or trust is broken, you aren't just saying goodbye to the present moment—you're also letting go of hopes, plans, and identities tied up in that connection. Processing these intangible losses makes healing feel heavier. It's a grief layered with nostalgia, regret, and sometimes deep questions about self-worth and meaning. These bittersweet thoughts don't fit neatly into a checklist of emotions, which can leave you feeling stuck in a liminal space between past and future.

The fear of vulnerability often closes off the path to healing as well. Opening your heart after betrayal or loss feels risky because the wounds are raw and tender. It's instinctive to protect yourself by putting up walls, shutting down emotionally, or numbing pain through distractions and unhealthy habits. While these coping strategies might provide short-term relief, they complicate long-term healing by blocking the very feelings and processing needed to move through pain. Being vulnerable requires courage and trust—both in yourself and others—and rebuilding that trust after it's been shattered takes time and fierce determination.

Healing feels hard because it's not just about repairing a broken heart but about transformation. It asks you to integrate pain into your life story and find new meaning beyond the hurt. This process requires patience, kindness, and a willingness to face discomfort head-on. It invites you to become both the mourner and the healer, holding two truths at once: that you are deeply wounded and that you possess the resilience to recover. This dual role can feel overwhelming, but it's also where the seeds of growth and renewal lie.

Sometimes, the difficulty in healing arises because you're dealing with complex emotional layers all at once. Loss rarely comes in isolation. It can stir up old wounds, fears, and unresolved pain from the past, creating a complicated emotional stew that's hard to untangle. When multiple losses or betrayals accumulate, it's like carrying a heavier and heavier burden, and your energy to heal can feel depleted. Recognizing that this overload is part of the process can help you be more patient with yourself instead of pushing too hard or judging your progress.

Another subtle but powerful reason healing feels so hard involves our identity and sense of self. When someone we

loved betrays us or leaves, it can shake our very foundation—
the beliefs we've held about ourselves and the world. This can
trigger an internal crisis where you question who you are, what
you're worth, or whether you'll ever be whole again. Healing
means facing these existential questions without definitive
answers right away. It means learning to live with uncertainty
and rebuilding your self-image from the ground up. That's a
tall order for anyone.

Despite all these challenges, it's important to remember
that the difficulty of healing doesn't mean you won't get
through it. Each small step—each moment when you allow
yourself to feel, reflect, or simply breathe freely—is progress.
Healing is more like shelling an onion than wiping a slate
clean. Each layer you gently peel back reveals more about your
strength, complexity, and capacity to love and be loved. It's
messy, nonlinear, and often exhausting work, but it's also the
path forward toward rediscovering peace.

In essence, healing feels so hard because it asks you to
hold space for pain while simultaneously reaching for hope.
It demands bold self-compassion in the face of vulnerability,
rewiring your thoughts and emotions when patterns once
carved deep feel almost permanent. The struggle you experience
now is not a sign of failure but a signal of how profoundly
you're engaged in reclaiming your life and heart. This hard,
beautiful, raw process is where resilience is born, and where
your story of transformation begins to take shape.

Myths About Grief, Time, and "Moving On"

When someone experiences heartbreak or loss, there's an unspoken expectation from others—and sometimes ourselves—that grief should follow a neat timeline. People often say, "Time heals all wounds," or, "You just need to move on." But these phrases, as comforting as they might seem, can confuse and even isolate us during our most vulnerable moments. The reality is far more complex. Grief refuses to fit into tidy boxes, and the journey toward healing doesn't follow a straight path. Understanding the myths around grief, time, and moving on is crucial for anyone struggling with emotional pain.

One common myth is that grief lasts only a certain amount of time. You might hear, "It's been six months—shouldn't you be over it by now?" These kinds of statements not only pressure you to "get better" on a schedule but also shame you for feeling deeply longer than expected. Grief doesn't work like a clock ticking down to zero. Sometimes, it isn't even linear. Some days it feels manageable, and other days it swells unexpectedly, catching you off guard. The idea that there's a deadline for feeling sad can make you doubt your own experience, which is the last thing anyone needs.

Another pervasive myth is that "moving on" means forgetting. This couldn't be further from the truth. Moving on doesn't mean erasing what you've lost or pretending the pain wasn't real. Instead, it involves integrating your experience into your life in a way that still honors the depth of your pain while allowing you to find space for new chapters. When people tell you to stop dwelling on the past, they may mean well, but it often comes across as dismissive. Grief isn't about forgetting; it's about learning to live with the pieces left behind in a new way.

There's also the mistaken belief that grief should look the same for everyone. That somehow, the process is uniform and predictable. In truth, grief is deeply personal and can express itself through a mix of emotions like anger, numbness, guilt, or even relief. The length and intensity of grief vary widely, depending on many factors—your relationship with what or who was lost, your personal coping mechanisms, and your support system. Some people cry daily for months, others may appear calm but feel turmoil underneath. Neither experience is a measure of your strength or the genuineness of your sadness.

People also tend to think that one should eventually "put the past behind" and stop talking about the loss. But silencing the pain too soon can trap it inside, making healing more difficult, not easier. Sharing your story, expressing your feelings, and even revisiting painful memories are essential steps that allow wounds to breathe. Avoiding your pain doesn't speed up recovery—it creates layers of unresolved emotion that keep you stuck. Healing asks you to make peace not by erasing the past, but by acknowledging it honestly.

Time is often seen as the magic ingredient to heal emotional wounds. While time is a necessary factor, it's not a cure by itself. Simply waiting doesn't guarantee that grief will weaken or disappear. Time can provide perspective, yes. But healing also requires active engagement—to process feelings, seek support, and take steps toward self-kindness. Time without these elements might just be a stretch of endurance rather than true recovery. Far from an automatic fix, healing tends to be messy, unpredictable, and ongoing.

What about the pressure to "stay strong"? This myth suggests that showing vulnerability or breaking down is a sign of weakness. In reality, embracing the pain openly is a courageous act and a critical part of healing. Hiding your tears or burying your hurt only delays facing the hurt that demands attention. Strength isn't about ignoring the ache; it's found in the willingness to feel deeply and keep moving forward despite it.

There's also a dangerous myth that grief must look like sadness. While sadness is a core part of grief, it's rarely the full story. You might feel relief, confusion, anger, shame, or even moments of unexpected joy. These mixed emotions can feel conflicting, leading to self-judgment or guilt. But grief is a complex emotional landscape. Allowing space for all the feelings that arise prevents you from falling into the trap of thinking your grief isn't "right" or valid if it doesn't fit the expected mold.

And what about the idea that forgiving yourself and others quickly leads to moving on? Forgiveness is often misunderstood as a quick fix, something to check off a list to hasten healing. But forgiveness is a process, not an event, and it doesn't mean you have to forget what happened or excuse harmful behavior. Sometimes, forgiveness means setting boundaries and reclaiming your own power rather than simply absolving the other person. Rushing to forgive can actually cut short a much-needed phase of self-reflection and healing.

The myth that you have to do grief alone is one that makes the journey unnecessarily harder. There's often a stigma attached to asking for help or admitting that the pain feels overwhelming. But reaching out to friends, family, or professionals doesn't weaken you—it strengthens you. Sharing your burden lightens the load and reminds you that you're not isolated in your suffering. Healing thrives in connection because emotional wounds can't fully mend in silence.

Finally, many believe that moving on means you'll suddenly "feel better" and life will return to normal. The truth is, life after loss often looks very different than before. Moving on means adjusting to a new reality, one where the loss is woven into your story but no longer dominates it. It doesn't mean a permanent absence of hurt but a gradual realignment where you can carry your pain alongside hope, purpose, and growth. These shifts happen over time, sometimes imperceptibly, yet powerfully.

Understanding these myths helps us approach grief with more grace and patience. When you stop expecting grief to follow rules and timelines, you give yourself permission to heal in your own way. This shift frees you from unnecessary guilt and frustration and opens the door to a gentler, more compassionate healing journey. Remember, grief is a deeply human experience, chaotic and tender—and it's okay to take as long as you need to find your peace.

CHAPTER 2

THE JOURNEY INWARD

When everything feels shattered, the idea of turning inward can seem both daunting and necessary—this chapter invites you to step gently into that space with courage and kindness. It's about giving yourself full permission to experience every emotion without judgment, even the ones that sting or embarrass you, because healing starts not when you push pain away but when you welcome it as part of your story. Naming what broke you helps uncloud the confusion, making the invisible wounds visible, while quieting the relentless inner critic opens the door to self-compassion. Here, letting go isn't about erasing what happened but releasing the grip of blame and resentment so you can breathe freely again. This inward journey might feel like walking through a storm, but beyond it lies the stillness where true forgiveness exists— not as forgetting or excusing, but as reclaiming your peace and power. Embracing this path honors both the heartbreak and the hope that lies ahead.

Giving Yourself Permission to Feel

The moment you experience heartbreak, loss, or betrayal, an immediate and often overwhelming tide of emotions can crash over you. It's tempting to push those feelings aside—after all, society tends to celebrate strength by promoting emotional control or stoicism. But holding back your feelings, denying their presence, or trying to sweep them under the rug only prolongs the struggle. Giving yourself permission to feel isn't just a suggestion; it's a radical act of self-love and the first real step toward healing.

When people talk about emotional pain, they often mean the anguish, sorrow, anger, or confusion that follows a devastating event. But what they don't always understand is how vital it is to actually sit with those feelings rather than running from them. Each emotion—no matter how raw or uncomfortable—carries information. It's your inner self's way of communicating what needs attention and care. Granting yourself permission to feel means you honor that communication instead of dismissing it.

Fear of feeling too much is one of the main reasons we hold back. What if sadness consumes you? What if anger spirals out of control? Or what if your grief turns into something so heavy you never rise from it? These are normal fears and worries. But experience shows that the opposite is true. When you allow yourself to lean into emotion without judgment or resistance, you begin to weaken its grip. The feelings lose their power to control you because they're no longer bottled up or running silent beneath the surface.

Giving yourself this permission might sound simple in theory, but in practice, it often takes courage. You might have been taught from a young age that showing pain is a sign of weakness, or that pushing forward means ignoring your feelings. Maybe you've labeled yourself as "too sensitive" or "overreacting." These messages can become internal scripts that shut down emotional openness. Reclaiming your right to feel is about breaking free from those scripts and rewriting the story about what strength really means.

Consider the difference between feeling and being consumed by feeling. They're not the same, though at times they may seem indistinguishable. Feeling means you recognize the wave of emotion present in you and allow it to pass through your awareness. Being consumed means you get pulled under by the tide, losing track of who you are underneath it all. The key is mindful permission: you acknowledge your pain without letting it define or drown you. This balanced approach creates a space for healing to begin, even if that space feels shaky at first.

Allowing yourself to feel also means rejecting the cultural urge to "fix" yourself quickly or numb out the pain. Whether through distractions, substances, or forcing a premature "move on," short-circuiting your emotional process delays genuine healing. Instead, leaning into your feelings invites the body and mind to fully experience and then soften around whatever you're holding. The tears, anger, and sorrow—they're the language your heart uses to communicate loss. Listening without judgment is a powerful form of kindness.

Sometimes, giving yourself permission to feel demands setting boundaries with others. When you're coping with heavy emotions, social pressures might push you to appear "fine" or avoid certain topics. It's okay to say no to conversations or interactions that don't honor where you are emotionally. Protection of your emotional landscape is part of honoring your feelings. You don't have to justify or explain why you need space; simply recognizing your limits and acting on them is an important form of self-respect.

One of the most common barriers to permission is the inner critic's voice. This internal dialogue often tells you to "get over it," "stop being dramatic," or "just move on already." Those toxic messages prevent you from accepting your pain as valid. If you listen to and challenge this inner critic, you start creating a new habit—one where your emotional responses are met with compassion instead of blame. This shift is vital. It changes your relationship with your emotions from enemy to ally, making the journey inward less daunting.

It's also important to remember that feeling deeply isn't limited to sadness or anger. You might encounter moments of guilt, shame, loneliness, or confusion, all of which are difficult but necessary to face. You may even experience feelings of emptiness or numbness, which are your heart's way of protecting you from further hurt. Each of these emotional states deserves acknowledgment. By giving yourself permission to feel, you validate even the hardest-to-face emotions.

Accepting your feelings without apology doesn't mean you have to act on every impulse or let your emotions run wild. There's strength in discernment too. You can experience your feelings fully while choosing thoughtful, constructive ways to respond. Maybe you cry alone, journal your thoughts, or talk to someone you trust. You might practice deep breathing or spend time in nature to ground yourself. These acts are all ways of honoring your feelings without becoming overwhelmed by them.

This permission to feel goes beyond individual moments. It's about giving yourself ongoing space to be human, to not "get it right" all the time, and to allow healing at its own pace. Some days will bring heavy waves of sorrow, and others might offer brief respite and lightness. Neither the dark nor the light cancels out the other. Both are part of your emotional landscape, and both deserve recognition and respect.

Sometimes the hardest part is letting go of the story that you have to hurry through pain or fix it before it defines you. Healing asks you to pause, to lean in, and to sit with your emotions without rushing. The paradox is clear: permission to feel is what eventually sets you free. Without it, the heart remains trapped by fear and confusion, unable to move toward peace.

When you give yourself permission to feel, you also cultivate patience and gentleness. Instead of beating yourself up for "still feeling this way," you acknowledge that healing often unfolds in a non-linear way. Feelings ebb and flow, rise and fall, sometimes surprising you when you least expect them. This is normal. This is real. This is you learning to live authentically again.

Remember that your feelings don't make you weak; they make you human. In fact, the courage to face your pain head-on is one of the strongest things you can do. It's what opens the door to deeper understanding, resilience, and ultimately, peace. So when the tide of emotion rolls in, don't fight it. Give yourself permission to feel, fully and unapologetically. It's the beginning of your journey inward—the start of reclaiming your heart's sacred healing.

Embracing Emotions Without Shame

One of the most challenging parts of healing after a heartbreak, loss, or betrayal is learning to accept your feelings fully—without judging yourself or pushing those emotions away. Society often teaches us to hide our pain or "be strong" by pretending things don't affect us deeply. But real strength lies in embracing every feeling that rises within you, no matter how messy, confusing, or painful it may seem.

If you've ever caught yourself thinking, "I shouldn't feel this way," or "I'm too emotional," you're not alone. Shame has a sneaky way of making us believe that our emotions aren't valid or that expressing them is a sign of weakness. But shame only tightens the wounds already aching inside you. When you allow yourself to feel without shame, you begin to break that cycle. It's okay to feel broken, sad, angry, or lost. These emotions are evidence that you're human—they are not flaws or failures.

The act of embracing your emotions is also an act of self-respect. When you acknowledge what's going on inside you, you're telling yourself that your experience matters. It's like giving your heart permission to breathe, to be seen without filters or masks. This kind of acceptance creates space for healing, for gentleness, and for growth. And it all starts with allowing your feelings to exist openly, as they are.

Embracing emotions doesn't mean you have to stay overwhelmed by them. It means you give yourself the room to recognize the depth of your pain while also trusting that you will eventually find your way through it. There's no need to rush or pressure yourself to "get over it" quickly. Healing is deeply personal and can often feel like two steps forward, one step back. But leaning into your feelings without shame brings clarity over time—it helps you understand the roots of your pain and what you truly need.

Why do we feel shame about our emotions in the first place? A lot of it comes down to cultural conditioning. From a young age, many of us are taught to hide vulnerability, especially in moments of suffering. Boys might be told to "man up," while girls could hear that crying is "too much." These messages teach us to disconnect from our inner emotional landscape instead of exploring it. Unfortunately, burying pain doesn't erase it; it just stores it away, often making the hurt louder and more confusing.

When you begin to embrace emotions without shame, you start dismantling those old, harmful beliefs. You challenge the idea that feeling deeply makes you fragile or unworthy.

Instead, you cultivate a new understanding: your emotions are signals, messengers showing you what your heart needs attention on. When you honor them, you step closer to healing than you ever could by ignoring or suppressing those feelings.

Let's consider what this looks like in a practical sense. Imagine a moment when sadness wells up inside you—maybe triggered by a memory or a quiet moment alone. Instead of pushing it away or distracting yourself, try sitting with it for a few minutes. Notice the sensations—the heaviness, the ache in your chest, the tears that might fall. Don't label it as "bad" or something to be ashamed of. Instead, silently say to yourself, "This feeling is part of my story right now, and that's okay."

With practice, this simple acknowledgment can change your entire relationship to your emotions. You move from fighting against pain to walking alongside it. That shift creates less internal resistance, and paradoxically, less pain. When your emotions don't have to fight for survival, they can be processed, understood, and transformed.

This process also teaches you patience—with yourself and your healing journey. The moments when grief feels overwhelming won't last forever, even if it doesn't seem that way. When you face your emotions without shame, those intense waves eventually settle into calm waters, revealing new insights about your resilience and capacity for love, even in the aftermath of heartbreak.

Embracing your emotions gently but firmly can lead to self-discovery, too. It's easy to get lost in the story of what went wrong or who hurt you. But beneath that surface lies a spectrum of feelings waiting to be met—fear, hope, longing, and sometimes surprise at how strong you really are. You'll likely uncover parts of yourself you might have ignored or doubted. This newfound self-awareness is a source of power, fueling your healing in ways you may not expect.

Shame thrives in the shadows, but emotions, when embraced openly, lose their power to isolate you. They connect you—first to your own truth, then to others who have walked similar paths. When you're willing to show up for your emotions honestly, you invite empathy and compassion into your life, both from within and from those around you.

Of course, embracing emotions without shame doesn't mean you have to carry these feelings alone. Sharing your pain with trusted friends, family, or therapists can help break down the walls of isolation shame builds. Talking about your feelings, expressing them through writing or creative outlets, or simply sitting quietly with your emotions can all support this crucial step toward healing.

It's important to remember: emotions are neither good nor bad—they just are. They don't define you, but they do reflect a part of your experience. Allowing yourself to feel fully shows tremendous courage. It means you're willing to face the broken pieces of your heart with kindness rather than fighting against their existence.

This kind of radical acceptance is at the heart of emotional recovery. It lays the foundation for everything that follows in the healing journey—from naming your pain clearly, to silencing the harsh inner critic, to ultimately reclaiming joy and peace. But none of it can happen without embracing your emotions first, without giving them value and space.

So if you find yourself resisting sadness, anger, or fear, take a moment. Breathe deeply. Remind yourself that these feelings are part of your story—parts worth hearing. Replace the voice of shame with one of compassion. This small but profound shift will carry you through the darkest moments and lead you toward light, step by step.

Your emotions are not your enemy. They are your allies on this journey inward, guiding you toward healing, wholeness, and the peace your heart longs for. Embrace them without shame, and you'll discover the strength you've always had dwelling quietly within you.

Naming What Broke You

Facing emotional pain means facing the parts of ourselves that have been shattered, and that process begins with naming what broke you. It's a step that's deceptively simple but profoundly difficult. Naming isn't just about labeling the event, the person, or the circumstance that caused the hurt. It's about recognizing and owning the deep fracture within your heart and soul. When you give a name to your pain, you bring it out of the shadows and into the light, where healing can begin.

For many, the impulse to avoid naming their pain is powerful. Sometimes it feels safer to keep wounds vague or unnamed, as if ignoring the break might make it less real or less painful. But pain left unnamed tends to fester in silence, creating invisible chains that bind you to the past. Naming is the brave act of stepping into the discomfort, of saying aloud— or at least in your own heart—"This is what happened. This is what hurt me." It's not about blame but about acknowledgment.

When you name your pain, you start pulling apart the tangled emotions that swirl inside. Is it loss? Betrayal? Abandonment? Trust broken or dreams deferred? Each of these words carries a different weight, a different kind of aching. Naming helps sort through the confusion and chaos so you can understand what's truly at the root of your suffering. This clarity is an essential first step toward reclaiming your power.

Many people hesitate to name the pain because it forces a confrontation with feelings they might not fully understand or don't feel ready to face. There's vulnerability in revealing what broke you. However, vulnerability is not weakness—it is strength in its most honest form. When you begin to say the words that describe your hurt, you take back control. You stop being defined by the silence around your experience and begin defining your relationship with that pain on your own terms.

Some wounds are collective in nature—a break caused by breach of trust in a relationship, a sudden loss, or a profound betrayal. Naming these hurts ties your personal story to the shared human experience of suffering. This connection reminds you that you're not alone, even in your darkest moments. The pain may be deeply personal, but the act of naming it creates a bridge to others who have walked, and are walking, that same difficult path.

It's also important to recognize that naming what broke you is not a one-time event but an evolving process. Sometimes, the name changes as you uncover more layers within yourself. What seemed like heartbreak can reveal aspects of abandonment or suppressed grief. You might discover anger buried beneath sadness or fear underlying shame. This unfolding self-awareness is a sacred dialogue with your inner world. It invites you to keep looking, keep questioning, and keep feeling without judgment.

The fear of being overwhelmed by the pain once it's named is real and common. But rather than swelling uncontrollably, this kind of naming often brings a kind of release. Like admitting a secret aloud, the hurt loses some of its mysterious power. It is no longer a silent, creeping shadow, but a named presence you begin to understand and gently face. This shift can reduce anxiety and the sense of being helplessly trapped by your emotions.

When you put words to the breakage, you're also creating language to tell your story later—whether to yourself or others. Language frames your experience and shapes your healing narrative. Without it, your pain remains fragmented and unreal, slipping through the cracks of memory and feeling. With it, the story becomes whole. It can be told, retold, reshaped, and eventually released.

Consider, too, that naming what broke you doesn't fix the wound instantly. It's not a magic cure. Instead, it's the foundation—you're building a house you can eventually live in again. You need a sturdy foundation before you can raise the walls or open the windows. For many, the courage to name their pain is the first solid brick in the architecture of rebuilding their inner lives.

At times, you might find the words "broken," "shattered," or "fractured" resonate deeply. These terms acknowledge the rawness of your experience without minimizing it. Other times, the words might feel too heavy or absolute. You can choose gentler language that feels right for where you are in your journey—phrases like "cracked" or "in pieces" may capture your experience better. The important part is honesty with yourself. Don't rush this process or expect perfection. Your language can grow and shift as you heal.

One significant barrier to naming what broke you is the internal critic that whispers things like "You shouldn't feel this way" or "It's not that bad." These voices can cloud your ability to fully identify your pain. When you hear these doubts, remember that naming is a deeply personal and validating act. It's about naming your experience exactly as it is for you, not how you think it should be seen or measured by others. Your pain deserves respect and witnesses, starting with your own self.

Sometimes, the story behind your breakage might feel too complex to untangle alone. In these moments, finding compassionate support—a friend, therapist, or trusted guide—can help you find the right words when you feel stuck. Talking about what broke you out loud can start to dissolve the isolation around your pain. Often, healing begins from letting yourself be heard without judgment.

What you're really doing through naming is giving your fragmented heart a voice. You're acknowledging the parts of yourself that were hurt, wounded, or betrayed. This voice becomes the first step toward befriending the brokenness rather than resisting it. It invites a gentler, more curious relationship with your suffering where healing can take root.

In essence, naming what broke you is an act of courage and kindness toward yourself. It's a way of telling your soul, "I see you. I see the pain you carry. I'm here for you." This is the strongest foundation for all the healing work that follows. When you move forward from this place, the rest of the journey inward becomes clearer and more compassionate.

So take this step without pressure or hurry. Let your heart speak its truth in its own time. Whatever name you find for your pain will lead you forward, closer to peace with your broken pieces.

Honoring the Story Behind the Pain

When we think about healing from emotional pain, it's tempting to rush past the story—the why and the how—and jump straight to feeling better. But the truth is, the story behind your pain isn't just background noise. It's part of the very fabric of your experience, the thread that connects your heartbreak to your healing. Honoring that story means giving space to everything you've endured without judgment or rush, allowing yourself to fully encounter the truth of what happened.

Every emotional wound carries a story that deserves to be heard, even if it's painful, confusing, or messy. Sometimes the story is about love lost in the blink of an eye; other times, it's about betrayal that shook your foundation to its core. Maybe it's the quiet ache of unnoticed grief, or the sharp sting of rejection. Whatever form it takes, your story is unique—no one else has lived your exact experience. To honor it, you'll have to sit with it, not as a way to relive the hurt endlessly, but to understand and validate what it means to you.

It's important to recognize that honoring your story doesn't mean you're stuck in the past. Instead, it's an active, compassionate choice to lean into your truth before moving on. There's power in this because when you deny the reality of your pain or try to minimize it, you risk suppressing parts of yourself that need attention and care. Those parts can linger under the surface, quietly sabotaging your peace and making the healing process much slower and more complicated.

Think of your pain as an old wound on your soul. If you ignore it, it doesn't just disappear. It festers. It grows infected with shame, doubt, or anger. But when you choose to honor that wound—acknowledging it without trying to fix it immediately—you begin the process of true healing. This often means giving yourself permission to feel deeply, to cry, to rage, or to simply sit in the ache. These emotions are not obstacles but necessary steps toward reclaiming your wholeness.

Honoring your story also means reclaiming your narrative from anyone who tried to rewrite it for you. Maybe people told you to "get over it," "stop being so sensitive," or "look on the bright side." Those voices are common, but they don't hold your truth. Your pain is real, and your experience deserves respect. When you affirm your story, you push back against the harmful narratives that can try to silence your healing or confuse your sense of self.

There is something deeply transformative about facing your story head-on. When you tell it, whether in journaling, conversation, or quiet reflection, you bring clarity to a chaotic internal world. Your feelings become less overwhelming because they're named and understood. The murky memories start to take shape, making it easier to grasp the lessons hidden within the loss or betrayal. And as you gain insight, the story shifts from a trap to a gateway—the painful parts become not just reasons for suffering but parts of your growth.

One of the most significant ways to honor your story is to release any shame that clings to it. Shame tells you that something is wrong with you, that your pain is a sign of weakness or failure. But this couldn't be further from the truth. Pain is a universal human experience—it doesn't mean you're broken or unworthy. In fact, choosing to face your story bravely is a testament to your courage and resilience. It's a radical act of self-love to say, "This happened to me, and I am still here."

Honor also means being patient and gentle with yourself throughout this process. You might find that your story twists and turns as you revisit it. Feelings may come up that surprise or unsettle you. This is normal. Healing isn't linear. You might take two steps forward and one step back—sometimes much more. That's okay. Your story is not a problem to solve quickly but a journey to unfold over time. Giving yourself grace in this way honors the depth and complexity of what you're going through.

As you honor your story, you may notice the small truths buried inside moments of pain—truths about your needs, your strengths, and your values. A breakup might reveal your capacity for deep love even when it wasn't reciprocated. Betrayal might highlight your boundaries and the importance of protecting your heart. Loss might make you aware of your resilience and your ability to find meaning even in sorrow. These truths become part of the foundation on which you build your healing.

This section of your inward journey also invites you to practice presence with your pain. That means not running from it or distracting yourself but allowing your attention to rest evenly on the whole story, both the beautiful parts and the hard parts. This might seem counterintuitive or even scary at first. Our instinct is often to avoid pain, but when you offer it your full attention, you dismantle its power over you. The story stops controlling you because you've met it with openness.

Honoring the story behind the pain connects directly to self-compassion. When you treat your experience with kindness, you create an internal environment where healing can thrive. It's easy to be harsh and critical when you're hurting, especially if your inner critic likes to replay the parts of your story where you feel you "failed" or "didn't do enough." But practicing self-compassion during this phase reminds you that you're human, vulnerable, and worthy of care no matter what happened. It's about being your own ally during the hardest parts of your journey.

Another important aspect of honoring your story is recognizing it as a sacred part of your identity rather than a label that confines you. It's tempting to define yourself solely by what you suffered—the "heartbroken," "betrayed," or "grieving" person. But your story includes much more than your pain. Healing comes when you embrace the entire narrative, allowing yourself the freedom to grow beyond the chapters written by loss and heartbreak. This perspective shifts the story from something that limits you to something that enriches your understanding of who you are.

Sometimes, the process of honoring your story might bring up a paradoxical mix of emotions—relief and sadness, gratitude and anger, hope and despair. All of these feelings are valid and can coexist. Healing doesn't erase difficult emotions; it teaches you to hold them all with kindness and curiosity. This integration is what makes your inward journey genuine and transformative rather than superficial.

In the quiet moments when you reflect on your story, consider what you might say to your past self if you could step back in time. What words would you offer? What comforts would you provide? This exercise isn't about changing history but about creating a dialogue between who you were then and who you are now. You're essentially becoming a witness to your own journey, offering the compassion and understanding you needed when the pain first arrived.

Honoring the story behind your pain helps dismantle the isolation often felt in emotional turmoil. When you recognize that your story holds meaning and deserves attention, you create a bridge between yourself and others who have walked similar paths. This connection can be incredibly healing, reminding you that although your experience is unique, you are not alone in your suffering.

Ultimately, this phase of The Journey Inward calls you to embrace your story fully—its fractures, its truths, and its healing potential. It's an act of courage, humility, and profound self-respect. By honoring the story behind the pain, you lay the groundwork for the next steps forward with newfound strength and authenticity. Your heart is in pieces now, but through this honoring, those pieces become the mosaic of your healing.

Silencing the Inner Critic

When heartbreak strikes, it's almost inevitable that a harsh voice inside starts whispering—or sometimes shouting—doubt, shame, and blame. This voice is the inner critic, that relentless echo of negativity that chips away at your self-worth just when you feel weakest. It's a familiar tormentor that says you should have done more, been stronger, or simply been better. But in the journey inward, learning how to silence this inner critic is one of the most crucial steps toward healing and reclaiming peace.

The inner critic often operates under the guise of protection. It's that part of you trying to prevent further pain by pointing out mistakes, rehearsing what went wrong, or anticipating future hurts. It wants you to believe you're at fault, that your pain is evidence of personal failure. But here's the truth: the inner critic thrives on your suffering. It feeds the cycle of shame and anxiety, trapping you in a spiral that makes recovery feel impossible. Understanding this dynamic is the first shake needed to loosen its grip.

Silencing the inner critic doesn't mean ignoring it or pretending it's not there. In fact, dismissing or suppressing this voice tends to give it even more power. Instead, it's about recognizing when those critical thoughts enter, acknowledging them without judgment, and choosing not to follow where they lead. It's a practice—a process—of building awareness. You begin to see these negative thoughts for what they really are: automatic, learned patterns rather than absolute truths.

One practical way to start this process is by naming the critic when it shows up. Giving it a voice, even a silly nickname, helps create some distance and makes it less intimidating. When you hear, "You're not good enough," respond, "That's the critic talking, not me." This simple acknowledgment reveals the critic as a separate entity with its own agenda. Over time, the grip that voice holds lessens.

Another powerful tool is curiosity. Ask yourself why the inner critic is so loud right now? What fear or unmet need is beneath its words? Often, this voice emerges from deep vulnerabilities—a fear of rejection, the pain of abandonment, or feelings of unworthiness. When you gently explore what's behind the criticism, you start addressing the real wounds instead of the surface-level insults. This is where healing subtly begins to replace self-judgment.

It's also important to remember that the inner critic only has as much power as you give it. Feeding it with attention, agreement, or emotional energy strengthens its hold. Instead, imagine it like a radio station that broadcasts constant distortion. You don't have to keep tuning in. Turning your focus to self-compassion, positive affirmations, or the simple act of breathing deeply can shift the channel. You reclaim control not by overpowering the critic but by redirecting your mind to something life-affirming.

Letting go of the critic doesn't mean you suddenly become immune to painful thoughts. They may still show up like uninvited guests, but now you greet them with kindness instead of fear. You realize these are just thoughts—not commands—and you can choose which ones deserve your attention. This shift might feel foreign at first, even uncomfortable. But with patience, it becomes easier to spot the difference between your true self and the voice trying to tear you down.

For many facing heartbreak, the inner critic often disguises itself in phrases like "I should have seen this coming," or "I'm the reason everything fell apart." These painful narratives erode trust in yourself and make healing feel distant. Challenging these beliefs means confronting deeply ingrained stories and replacing them with kinder truths. You might remind yourself that relationships end for countless reasons, many beyond your control, and that your worth isn't defined by this loss.

Practicing self-compassion is a key ally when silencing the inner critic. It's about speaking to yourself like you would to a trusted friend who's hurting. Instead of berating or blaming, you offer understanding and patience—even if you don't always feel like it. This gentle approach gradually softens the inner landscape, allowing room for growth and renewal. It creates a safety net for your heart to mend and for joy to return in its own time.

Keep in mind that the inner critic often grows louder because your emotional wounds are fresh and tender. It reacts out of fear, trying to protect you by warning of future disappointment or failure. But paradoxically, this protection feels like prison. Real security comes from learning to trust yourself again—your resilience, your ability to heal, your courage to face emotions fully. Silencing that critical voice is really about reclaiming that trust.

When you catch yourself spiraling into self-criticism, it can be helpful to pause and put those thoughts on trial. Ask, "Is this true? Where's the evidence?" Often, the critic exaggerates or distorts reality. Maybe one painful moment doesn't define your entire worth. Maybe you've survived worse and grown stronger. Reminding yourself of these truths weakens the critic's narrative and anchors you in reality rather than fear.

This process won't happen overnight. The inner critic is a stubborn presence, shaped by years of experience, social conditioning, and emotional pain. But every small act of resistance chips away at its power. Writing down negative thoughts and then writing compassionate responses can be a surprisingly effective practice. Over time, this creates a new internal dialogue—one that nurtures rather than punishes.

Remember also that you're not alone in this struggle. Almost everyone carries an inner critic, especially after deep emotional wounds. What's different now is your willingness to look inward, to gently question and transform that voice. This willingness speaks volumes about your courage and your commitment to healing. It's a quiet act of rebellion against despair and self-doubt.

Silencing the inner critic opens up space for your authentic self to emerge. It allows you to listen to your own needs, hopes, and desires without fear of judgment. When that critical voice quiets, it creates a fertile ground for self-compassion to take root. And from that compassion, true healing begins.

At the heart of it all lies a simple truth: you deserve kindness—from others and most importantly, from yourself. You deserve the grace to heal without harshness. As you journey inward, give yourself the permission to be imperfect, to stumble, to feel pain deeply, and still find tenderness within. That's the path forward, through the noise of the critic, toward the peace waiting quietly on the other side.

Replacing Self-Blame with Self-Compassion

When we're caught in the throes of emotional pain—whether it's from a breakup, a deep loss, or a betrayal—the tendency to blame ourselves feels almost automatic. The mind replays mistakes, perceived failures, and moments where things "should have" gone differently. This self-blame can seem like a form of control, like taking responsibility might somehow fix the broken pieces inside. But in truth, it keeps us stuck, tangled in a loop of guilt and shame that weighs heavily on the heart and dims the light of healing.

Replacing self-blame with self-compassion is not about dismissing responsibility or shirking accountability. It's about shifting the way we treat ourselves amid pain: from harsh judgment to kindness, from punishment to understanding. Imagine speaking to yourself like you would to a friend who's hurting—gently, patiently, without expectation or criticism. This change in inner dialogue is one of the most powerful steps you can take on your journey inward. It nurtures the soil where healing and growth can finally take root.

Self-blame often masquerades as a false form of strength—a belief that if we own all fault, maybe the pain won't swallow us whole. But carrying blame is a heavy burden that drains energy and narrows perspective. When you release blame, you're not giving up; you're making space for a broader, kinder understanding of your experience. This doesn't mean denying the pain or avoiding the truth. Rather, it means acknowledging your humanity—your limits, your efforts, and the fact that some outcomes are simply beyond control.

At the core of self-compassion is the recognition that everyone suffers and makes mistakes—and that this shared human experience connects us rather than separates us. When the inner critic shouts its tired accusations, self-compassion whispers back truths like: "You did the best you could with what you knew," or, "This pain is part of being human, not a sign of failure." These phrases, repeated over time, have the power to soften even the harshest self-judgments and open the door to forgiveness for yourself.

It's important to understand that learning self-compassion is a process, often requiring deliberate practice. In moments of acute hurt, reaching for compassionate self-talk might feel foreign or even impossible. That's okay. Start small—maybe by simply noticing the tone and content of your inner dialogue. Are you harsh or gentle? Are you supportive or critical? Awareness is the first step toward change.

Another key to this transformation is recognizing that self-blame often stems from unhealed wounds and unmet needs. If you find yourself drowning in "what ifs" or "if onlys," try to trace those feelings back to underlying fears—fear of being unworthy, unloved, or abandoned. These fears often drive the relentless self-accusations. By bringing them to light and addressing them with kindness, you can loosen their grip. It helps to ask yourself, "What do I need right now?" and then offer that to yourself in whatever form feels nourishing— whether it's rest, reassurance, or simply permission to be imperfect.

One way to cultivate self-compassion is to engage in what some call a "compassionate letter" exercise. Writing a letter to yourself from the perspective of a caring friend or mentor reminds you that you deserve the same empathy and encouragement you freely give to others. This isn't a one-time act, but rather a practice you can revisit as pain resurfaces. Over time, these messages build an internal support system that begins to drown out the inner critic's voice.

It also helps to remind yourself that emotional pain isn't a reflection of your worth or value—it's a signal that something in your life has shifted, that you've been deeply human in your experience. When you treat yourself with compassion, you honor not just your suffering, but your strength to continue moving forward despite it. This gentle attitude fosters resilience. It reminds you that healing isn't about perfection or speed; it's about showing up for yourself consistently, even on the hard days.

Self-compassion doesn't eliminate the sting of loss or the ache of betrayal, but it changes the way you relate to these experiences. The space created by compassion allows your heart to breathe, to hold grief without being crushed by it. You begin to see your story not as a series of failures but as chapters of growth. With time, this reframing brings a profound shift in how your pain integrates into the tapestry of your life.

Of course, the cultural messages we absorb—sometimes from a very young age—often encourage toughness over tenderness. It's no wonder then that turning inward with kindness can feel unfamiliar or even weak. But true strength lies in vulnerability. Being gentle with yourself during emotional upheaval is a radical act of courage that ultimately leads to liberation from suffering.

Engaging this process requires patience. You won't always succeed in quieting the voice of self-blame; it's persistent and skilled. But each time self-compassion shifts the narrative, even for a moment, it loosens the chains that bind you. Remember, this is a journey, not a destination.

It's also helpful to surround yourself with reminders of compassion outside your own mind. Whether it's books, music, conversations with caring people, or mindfulness practices, external affirmations can bolster your internal work. They reinforce the message that you're not alone in your struggles and that kindness—instead of blame—is your birthright.

When you embrace self-compassion, you aren't ignoring the reality of your pain or pretending everything is fine. Instead, you're choosing a pathway of radical acceptance that recognizes pain as part of the human condition. You give yourself permission to heal without judgment. This shift, as gradual as it might be, is a turning point. It frees up emotional energy that was once spent on self-criticism and opens the possibility of truly moving forward.

In this transformation, you reclaim your voice from the harsh inner commentaries that seek to diminish your worth. You begin to treat yourself as you deserve—with gentleness, kindness, and patience. And as you do, the fractured pieces of your heart can start to knit together not out of obligation or punishment, but out of genuine love and care for the person you are.

The Power of Letting Go

Letting go isn't about forgetting or pretending the pain never happened. It's much deeper and far more courageous than simply releasing what hurts. When your heart feels shattered from loss, betrayal, or heartbreak, holding on tightly to every fragment of the past can keep you locked in a prison of suffering. The power of letting go lies in the ability to free yourself from the chains of what was, so you can step fully into the present and open up to what's possible.

One of the hardest parts about letting go is the fear that doing so means giving up on love or hope. But holding on too tightly often means you're holding on to pain, resentment, or outdated stories that no longer serve your growth. These stories might whisper lies, convincing you that releasing is an act of weakness or abandonment. On the contrary, letting go requires tremendous strength. It is the willingness to embrace uncertainty and to trust life beyond what you can see or control.

You might wonder, how do you even begin to let go when the emotional weight feels unbearable? The journey starts with small, intentional steps. It isn't about erasing memories or feelings but allowing them the space to be felt, honored, and eventually transformed. Giving yourself permission to grieve and to remember without being trapped by pain opens a doorway to healing. It's like loosening your grip on a rope that's been tightened in fear—slowly, steadily, until you can release your grasp without falling.

The power of letting go also challenges the common misconception that healing is about "moving on" as if that means forgetting or replacing what you've lost. Healing doesn't ask you to erase the past; it invites you to integrate it—a process that requires patience, compassion, and time. What letting go really means is choosing to no longer let your past pain dictate your present or future. It's about reclaiming your narrative and realizing that peace isn't found in control, but in surrendering your need for it.

In moments of emotional turmoil, the heart clings to familiar pain because it feels safe in its known suffering. Pain can become a strange kind of comfort, a way we identify ourselves or protect ourselves from new wounds. Letting go is a radical act of self-love that breaks this cycle. It means daring to step beyond fear and anger, even when your heart protests. This isn't a linear process—sometimes you'll take steps forward, and other times it will feel like you're two steps back. That's okay. Every attempt at release weakens the hold pain has over you, even if it doesn't feel immediate.

When you let go, you also begin to loosen the grip of the stories you tell yourself about what happened. These narratives may have fueled self-blame, shame, or bitterness. Releasing these stories doesn't mean denying what was real; it means choosing not to let those narratives become the defining chapters of your life. You start to understand that your worth isn't rooted in your past suffering or the actions of others, but in your innate humanity and resilience.

It's often helpful to think of letting go as a process of making peace with paradox. You hold the pain and the possibility simultaneously. You honor your heartbreak but open yourself to joy again. You grieve but also find moments of grace. It's about balance—you acknowledge the past's impact while refusing to let it consume you. This act of balance invites a gentleness toward yourself that feels revolutionary when you've been hard on yourself throughout your suffering.

Practically speaking, letting go might look like setting boundaries that protect your emotional space, or consciously choosing to release grudges that anchor you to past hurts. Sometimes, it means forgiving not for the sake of others, but to unshackle yourself from bitterness. Other times, letting go involves embracing vulnerability enough to ask for help or express your truth openly. These steps may feel small, but each one chips away at the fortress pain builds around your heart.

The power of letting go also invites a radical trust in the process of life itself. When you release control—over people, outcomes, or emotions—you're stepping into a space where healing and transformation are possible. It doesn't happen overnight. There may be moments when grief resurfaces, or lost feelings return unexpectedly. Letting go is not about perfection but persistence; it's about returning to the intention to release again and again until the tie loosens.

Many who have walked through deep emotional pain find that once they embrace the power of letting go, they discover a new form of freedom—freedom that isn't dependent on circumstances but arises from within. It's a freedom to live with an open heart, even when life has been cruel. This is where true courage lives: in choosing hope and possibility over fear and pain.

Holding on can feel like survival, but letting go leads to thriving. It doesn't erase the heartbreak but transforms its hold over you. It allows you to gather the scattered pieces of your heart and rearrange them into something that carries both the scars and the strength you've earned. Letting go invites you to become the author of your healing story, in your own time and in your own way.

In unlocking the power of letting go, you reclaim your power, your peace, and ultimately, your capacity to love again—without losing yourself in the process. It is the doorway from being broken to being whole, wounded yet wondrously alive.

What Forgiveness Really Means (And Doesn't Mean)

Forgiveness is often misunderstood, especially when we're fresh from the raw edges of heartbreak, betrayal, or loss. It's easy to fall into the trap of thinking forgiveness means forgetting what happened or pretending the pain didn't exist. That's not what forgiveness is—and it's important to clarify that because holding onto the wrong definition can keep us stuck, feeling powerless and resentful.

At its core, forgiveness is a radical act of freedom. It means choosing to release the heavy weight of anger and pain you've been carrying—not for the person who hurt you, but for yourself. Forgiveness is about reclaiming your peace. It doesn't erase the past or justify the harm done to you, nor does it mean you're condoning that behavior. Instead, it's a deliberate decision to no longer let the wounds define how you live your life.

Many people who've been deeply hurt hesitate to forgive because they think it means they have to be best friends with the person who wronged them or open themselves up to getting hurt again. That's simply not true. Forgiveness isn't about reconciliation or offering an apology back to the offender. It's an internal process—you're forgiving because you need to heal. You deserve a heart that feels lighter and less burdened by the past.

What forgiveness absolutely is not is weakness. It isn't giving up your power or becoming a doormat. In fact, it takes enormous strength and courage to face your pain and say, "I'm done being defined by this." Forgiveness demands honest self-reflection and the willingness to confront difficult feelings without running away. It means standing in your truth, acknowledging the harm done, and deciding that your future won't be sabotaged by it.

Let me be clear: you don't have to forgive quickly, or ever if you're not ready. Forgiveness doesn't have a timeline. Sometimes, it feels impossible when your wounds are fresh and raw. That's okay. Forgiveness is a journey, not a switch you flip. It can take years, and sometimes it happens in tiny moments rather than big, sweeping epiphanies. The key is to keep moving toward it gently, without forcing yourself or indulging in bitterness.

One of the most challenging parts of forgiveness is dealing with the inner voices that insist you shouldn't forgive because it lets the other person "off the hook." Those voices echo the pain of betrayal. They're protective, but they also keep you caged in suffering. The truth is, forgiveness isn't about the other person's punishment or avoiding justice—it's about your liberation from emotional imprisonment.

When you decide to forgive, it doesn't mean you're forgetting the lessons you've learned. Forgiveness doesn't erase boundaries either. You can—and should—protect yourself from further harm. Learning to forgive while maintaining your safety and self-respect is a powerful paradox that many find difficult but profoundly freeing.

In the depths of emotional turmoil, forgiveness can feel like giving up, but it's the exact opposite. It's reclaiming your agency. Instead of being the person who was hurt, you become the person who chooses how to respond. Forgiveness is a means of shifting from victimhood toward empowerment, from pain to peace. It lets the heart breathe again.

So, how do you begin? It starts with permission—giving yourself permission to forgive without coercing your feelings. Acknowledging that forgiveness is a process tailored to your own pace helps reduce the pressure you might be feeling. Recognizing your emotions honestly—whether it's anger, sadness, or fear—is essential. Forgiveness doesn't ask you to bypass these feelings. Instead, it asks you to hold them with curiosity and kindness.

Another common misconception is that forgiveness requires a grand gesture or an incredible burst of willpower. While those moments can happen, forgiveness is often quiet and small. It happens in internal decisions, in releasing grudges during moments of calm, or in waking up each day with the intention to let go a little more. This cumulative practice creates a ripple effect, slowly transforming your pain into something lighter.

Forgiveness also means accepting your humanity—including your flaws. Holding onto resentment can often mask deeper feelings of shame or self-blame. Sometimes, forgiving others helps you forgive yourself too. Self-forgiveness is crucial on this path because it builds compassion that spills over into your relationships with others and the world. It rewires your heart to feel more openness instead of shutting down in protection.

It's important to remember that forgiveness can coexist with grief. Letting go of anger doesn't mean you stop mourning. You can hold sorrow and forgiveness side-by-side. That's part of the complexity of healing. Embracing this complexity can be freeing because it removes the demand to "fix" your emotions or rush to closure.

Forgiveness is also deeply personal. There's no one-size-fits-all formula. It can take many shapes—sometimes it's a silent prayer, sometimes journaling your feelings, sometimes simply a quiet choice made in the privacy of your thoughts. Whatever form it takes, true forgiveness is about the restoration of your emotional well-being more than meeting any external expectation.

In learning what forgiveness really means, you might discover new layers of strength you didn't know you had.

This strength builds resilience, helping you navigate future challenges with grace. People who have forgiven don't forget what they went through; they simply carry the lessons without the added weight of bitterness.

Ultimately, forgiveness is a gift you give yourself. It's a way of honoring your own worth and reclaiming your life from the hold of past hurt. It opens the door for peace to enter where pain once lived—a peace that doesn't erase your story but integrates it into a tapestry of growth, courage, and hope.

CHAPTER 3

REBUILDING FROM THE INSIDE OUT

Healing isn't about rushing through pain or plastering over cracks; it's about digging deep to rebuild the foundation beneath the broken pieces. Creating a safe space within yourself—where vulnerability meets strength—is the first step toward real restoration. Establishing new routines and clear boundaries helps protect that fragile, emerging self, allowing trust and love to grow again at a natural pace. This phase invites you to reconnect deeply with who you truly are, beyond the hurt and fear, and to open your heart slowly without rushing. As you release old wounds and fears, the journey moves from just surviving toward genuinely living, reclaiming joy and purpose that maybe felt distant before. Inside this process lies the powerful truth that your heart still knows how to love, and with compassionate intention, you can piece together a life that feels whole once more.

Creating Safe Spaces for Healing

When you're rebuilding from the inside out, one of the most vital steps is creating a safe space that nurtures healing. This space isn't always a physical place; it can be a mental realm, an emotional bubble, or a blend of both where you feel protected enough to be vulnerable. After experiencing heartbreak, loss, or betrayal, your heart and mind often feel raw and exposed, craving a sanctuary that offers both comfort and freedom from judgment. Without that protective space, healing tends to stall, or worse, you might find yourself resisting the very process that could help you feel whole again.

A safe space is essentially an environment where your truest feelings can emerge without fear. It's a place where you can honestly acknowledge the ache inside without minimization or pressure to 'fix' things immediately. At first, it may seem impossible to open up fully—even to yourself—for fear of drowning in the sorrow or anger. But creating safety is about setting the foundations to hold those emotions with kindness, not let them define or consume you. This takes intention, patience, and self-compassion. It means telling yourself it's okay to feel broken, that this is part of the journey and not a sign of weakness.

Think of the last time you felt emotionally unsafe— whether with others or alone. Maybe it was a moment when criticism felt overwhelming or when your thoughts spiraled out of control. Chances are, your body tightened, your heart raced, or you shut down altogether. That's your inner alarm signaling a need for protection. Part of creating this safe space involves learning to listen to those signals and respond gently. You don't have to force your heart open or push through the pain to heal; you can honor what you need at your pace. That may mean slowing down when the waves crash too heavily or choosing solitude until you regain strength.

Physical spaces often play a significant role in fostering safety. It could be a quiet corner in your home where you keep reminders of your progress—a journal, comforting objects, or soft lighting—that invite relaxation and reflection. Sometimes, rearranging your environment to feel calmer and more grounded can soothe the mind's chaos. Surrounding yourself with these simple anchors of peace creates a container for healing to unfold naturally. However, safe spaces don't require perfection or fancy setups. Even a few minutes of sitting somewhere peaceful, away from hustle and stress, can provide the pause your spirit needs.

Beyond physical surroundings, interpersonal relationships dramatically influence your sense of safety. After betrayal or loss, trust often feels fragile or broken, making it hard to rely on others. Choosing who you allow into your emotional space matters deeply. Safe spaces include people who listen without judgment, validate your feelings, and honor your boundaries. They don't rush your healing or try to "fix" you—rather, they sit with you in your messiness and uncertainty. These connections don't have to be numerous. One or two genuine allies who know how to hold your pain with respect and tenderness can make all the difference.

Boundaries form a crucial part of this sanctuary. They protect your energy and emotional well-being, especially when navigating turbulent feelings. Saying no to demands or conversations that trigger you isn't about shutting others out but about preserving your capacity to heal. Boundaries help you take ownership of your heart's needs rather than allowing external pressures to steer your journey. This could mean limiting contact with certain individuals, stepping back from social gatherings, or even temporarily unplugging from social media. These decisions create breathing room where your soul can breathe too.

Another layer of creating safety involves mindfulness—a gentle awareness of your present state without judgment. This practice invites you into your experience with curiosity rather than avoidance. When your heart feels shattered, it's tempting to push feelings down or distract yourself. But in a true safe space, you can explore what's arising moment by moment, witnessing your hurt and frustration as real but transient. Over time, this shifts your relationship with pain from being something to fear or escape to something you can sit beside with compassion and resilience. Mindfulness doesn't magically erase pain, but it softens its grip and invites healing energy.

Healing is also about permission—the permission you give yourself to be imperfect, confused, and slow. When you build a safe space, you acknowledge that healing isn't linear or tidy. It rarely moves in a straight line from broken to whole. Instead, expect days where the weight presses down, where tears come unbidden, or anger flares unexpectedly. These moments are not setbacks but vital parts of the process. A safe space embraces them without shame or self-recrimination. It encourages you to hold your own hand and whisper, "It's okay. You're doing the best you can."

Creating this sanctuary means dismantling the harsh inner critic that often takes center stage after emotional trauma. That voice tends to tell you that you're weak, inadequate, or that you should be "over it" by now. Safe spaces don't allow that voice to dominate. Instead, they invite an inner ally—one that reminds you that healing takes time and that your worth isn't tied to how quickly you recover. It encourages you to speak to yourself with the same gentleness you'd offer a close friend who's struggling. This nurturing inner dialogue helps build emotional resilience, making it easier to face painful moments without collapsing under their weight.

Sometimes, the safest space you can create isn't static but fluid—a shifting landscape where you meet yourself exactly where you are today. One day, it might be found in a quiet morning walk surrounded by nature's calm. Another day, it might be journaling your pain to a page that listens without interrupting. On harder evenings, it might mean simply breathing through the ache and reminding yourself this too shall pass. These changing practices reflect the reality that healing lives in motion, evolving alongside your feelings and needs. The key is that each step nurtures safety, not pressure; openness, not defensiveness.

Our culture often glorifies 'moving on' quickly, but healing isn't about erasing the past or pretending it never happened. It's about allowing yourself the freedom to rebuild from the inside, piece by piece, with kindness as your foundation. Creating safe spaces for healing means you stop forcing progress on your own terms and instead create an environment where healing naturally arises at its own right time. It's a radical act of self-love to carve out this sacred ground in a world that frequently demands you move faster than your heart is ready.

To rebuild from the inside out, honor your need for rest, protection, and understanding. In doing so, you transform from a survivor to a healer capable of deep renewal. Remember that safety isn't about never feeling pain again but about having an inner refuge where pain can coexist with hope. Building these safe spaces is a courageous act—it says you deserve care, tenderness, and kindness. And once you've anchored that sanctuary within, you'll find yourself ready to embrace the next chapter with newfound strength and grace.

Routines, Rituals, and Boundaries That Support You

When you're rebuilding from within, feeling safe and steady often hinges on the small, intentional practices woven into each day. Routines anchor us. They create a sense of predictability in a life that might otherwise feel scattered or out of control. After emotional turmoil—whether from heartbreak, loss, or betrayal—finding these anchors becomes vital. They don't erase the pain, but they provide a steady rhythm that can cradle your spirit as you heal.

Establishing a routine doesn't mean creating a rigid schedule that drains your energy. Instead, it's about gently shaping your days with practices that nurture your well-being and offer a sense of normalcy. Think of these as little acts of kindness toward yourself. Maybe it's starting your morning with deep breaths, stretching, or sitting quietly with a cup of tea before the world demands your attention. These seemingly small moments accumulate and can deeply affect how you experience the rest of your day.

Rituals, on the other hand, carry meaning beyond the practical. They serve as ceremony for your healing process— whether it's lighting a candle in the evening to honor your feelings, writing down what you're grateful for, or moving your body in a way that feels freeing. Rituals help us mark transitions, feel seen by ourselves, and reconnect with our own hearts. They remind us that healing isn't a destination; it's an ongoing, active journey. Creating your own rituals can also restore a sense of control when life seems unpredictable.

Boundaries are another powerful tool in the rebuilding process. When your heart is broken or your trust has been shaken, you need to protect the fragile space within you that's learning how to breathe again. This means saying no to things—people, situations, or even thoughts—that don't serve your peace. Boundaries aren't about being unkind or shutting people out forever; they're about honoring your needs and giving yourself permission to heal without unnecessary disruption.

One of the hardest parts of setting boundaries can feel like disappointing others or appearing "too fragile." But the truth is, boundaries communicate respect for your own emotional health, and they set the stage for healthier relationships down the line. They teach you how to stand firm in your worth, even when everything else feels shaky. You might have to experiment a bit, adjusting your limits to find what truly preserves your energy and encourages growth. Over time, these boundaries become both shield and bridge—a way to protect yourself and invite in connection on your terms.

As you put routines, rituals, and boundaries into place, it's important to remain flexible and compassionate. Some days will feel easier than others, and that's expected. When you slip or need to recalibrate, give yourself permission to do so without judgment. Healing isn't linear. Some mornings, your routine might look quite different because your needs have shifted, and that's okay. What matters most is that you stay connected to the intention behind these practices—the intention to nurture, protect, and rebuild.

Another aspect worth highlighting is that your routines and rituals should feel authentic to you. What nourishes one person may not work for another. Maybe meditation feels like sanctuary instead of coffee; maybe a walk in nature grounds you better than any mindfulness app. The key is to listen deeply to what your heart and body tell you they need right now, not what you think you should do or what worked in the past. Your healing process belongs to you, not anyone else's idea of what it "should" look like.

Boundaries often extend beyond external demands, too. Sometimes, we have to set limits on our own inner voices—the harsh self-critic that tends to flourish in the wake of emotional upheaval. Creating mental boundaries means learning to recognize when negative self-talk tries to take hold and gently redirecting it. Techniques like journaling, affirmations, or talking with a trusted friend or counselor can support this. By protecting your inner world from needless judgment, you foster an environment where compassion and kindness can grow.

In sum, these routines, rituals, and boundaries act like the scaffolding holding up your fragile emotional house while the rebuilding occurs. They create safe spaces within and around you—spaces that say, "Here is a place where your pain is honored, your needs are met, and your growth is possible." Without these supports, healing can feel overwhelming or impossible. With them, it becomes manageable, tangible, and full of potential.

And don't underestimate the power of consistency. Over time, even the smallest, daily acts of self-care and protection shape a new foundation beneath your feet. They remind you that you're worthy of tenderness, that your heart can soften again, and that the life waiting for you on the other side of pain can be rich and full—even if it looks different from before.

Lastly, hold on to hope in your routines. The very act of showing up for yourself, day after day, is an act of courage. It whispers to your soul that though you may be broken now, you are also whole enough to begin again. And, as this chapter emphasizes, the simple, intentional practices you cultivate will be the quiet yet powerful river beneath your journey—steady, sustaining, and endlessly patient.

Your Heart Still Knows How to Love

Even when heartbreak feels like it's swallowed you whole, your heart never actually forgets how to love. It might feel raw, cracked, or bruised, but beneath the surface, the capacity to open up and connect remains alive. It's easy to believe that after betrayal, loss, or intense emotional pain, your heart has shut its doors permanently. Yet love is more resilient than we give it credit for—it flickers quietly inside, waiting to be recognized again.

That quiet resilience is something to lean into, even if it's hard to feel at first. The heartbreak can make love feel like a distant memory rather than a present reality. You may wonder if you'll ever trust someone again, if you can really open yourself up without the fear of being shattered once more. This fear is natural, but it's also important to remember that your heart's ability to love is not dependent on who else shows up in your life. It's a gift you nurture within yourself first and foremost.

When you're deep in emotional turmoil, loving yourself can seem like an abstract concept or even an impossible task. The pain sometimes convinces you that you're unworthy or broken beyond repair. But these are not truths—they're the echoes of grief and shock that cloud your vision. Beneath all of that lies a core of you that deserves love, from yourself and from life. The challenge is learning to listen to this core without judgment, without rushing, and without forcing anything that doesn't feel genuine.

It helps to start with small acts of kindness toward yourself. These don't have to be grand gestures. It can be as simple as letting yourself rest when you're exhausted from emotional strain, or gently reminding yourself that it's okay to say no when something doesn't feel right. These small acts create a foundation—a way to prove to yourself that you matter. When you're able to witness your own worth, your heart's memory of love surfaces more clearly.

Love might feel like a foreign language right now, but it's one your heart speaks fluently. The key lies in finding ways to connect to it beyond the common expressions of romance or attachment. Sometimes we think of love only as being with someone else, but love has many forms. The love that heals begins as self-love—the kind of steady, unwavering care you give yourself through the pain. It's a love that looks like patience, acceptance, and gentle truth-telling.

It's also crucial to recognize that loving again doesn't mean erasing the past or pretending the pain didn't happen. It means allowing your heart to carry its history with grace and courage. Your heart grows wiser through the cracks; it understands tenderness and vulnerability in ways it never did before. It can hold grief and hope at the same time, and that dual capacity is what leads to genuine emotional rebirth. Love after loss is not the same love you had before, but it can be deeper and more grounded.

Fear of opening up again can cloud your perspective, whispering that protection means shutting down. But shutting down doesn't protect your heart; it numbs it. Building emotional walls might feel like keeping pain out, but it also blocks joy, connection, and growth. Love always involves some risk, yet the courage to be vulnerable again is an act of profound strength. Vulnerability isn't a weakness—it's the very place where healing and love intersect.

Give yourself permission to take things one step at a time. There's no schedule for how fast your heart should mend or how quickly you should trust again. Sometimes, loving again might start with loving a friend, your family, or even a pet—connections that remind you that affection and care still exist in the world. These experiences remind you that love doesn't have to be grandiose or perfect; it just has to be real and heartfelt.

It's in the little moments where your heart remembers most. A smile shared with a stranger, the warmth of sunlight on your skin, the soothing sound of your favorite song—these small instances can become gateways back to love. They remind you that the world is full of life-affirming experiences waiting to be noticed, even when you feel devastated inside.

Remember that learning to love after pain is also about patience. It's about acknowledging that setbacks and dark days are part of the process. Sometimes your heart will feel ready to trust again, only to pull back in fear the next day. This dance of giving and holding back is natural. Instead of judging yourself for it, see it as evidence of your complexity and emotional depth.

One of the most powerful ways to reconnect with love is by reconnecting with yourself. What makes you feel alive? What do you enjoy when no one else is watching? What small joys light you up, even on the hardest days? These questions help you rediscover your own heart's language, apart from the pain you've experienced. As you answer them, you'll find your inner voice becoming a source of comfort and guidance.

The heart's intuition about love is wise and trustworthy. It can sense when something is nurturing and when something is harmful. Honoring these instincts allows you to navigate relationships more safely and openly. You learn to set boundaries that protect your emotional well-being without shutting down your ability to connect. This balance is essential to rebuild a heart that loves bravely yet wisely.

Love doesn't demand perfection, and healing doesn't require a linear path. There will be days when your heart feels whole and joyful, and days when it shrinks inside from sadness or fear. All of this belongs to the journey. Your heart's capacity to love is tested and stretched, but never truly exhausted. It is a wellspring, always ready to flow again when you make space for it.

As you move forward, lean into the idea that your heart is not broken beyond repair. It's simply in the process of being redesigned—stronger, more resilient, and more compassionate. Love's ability to transform pain into growth is one of the most beautiful parts of the human experience. Even in the darkest seasons, your heart remembers how to open. It's ready to love again, for yourself and for others.

So, when doubt creeps in, remind yourself that you are not alone in this. Countless hearts have walked this path before you and found their way back to love. Your heart still knows how to love. It always has, and it always will.

Reconnecting with Yourself and Others

The path to healing after heartbreak or loss often feels like wandering through a dense fog—you know there's something on the other side, but the way isn't clear. One of the most vital steps in rebuilding yourself is to rekindle the connection not only with those around you but, most importantly, with your own inner self. Without this foundational reconnection, the sense of isolation and numbness can seem overwhelming, even permanent.

When pain strikes deeply, it's easy to retreat from the world and, at the same time, from yourself. You might notice your thoughts become harsher, your self-talk more critical, and your emotional responses dulled or explosive. This disconnect with your own feelings and needs can create a sense of being lost inside your own skin. The first step, then, is to listen closely to what your heart and body are whispering beneath the noise of grief.

Reconnecting with yourself doesn't happen overnight, nor is it a linear journey. It starts with small acts of presence— pausing to check in on how you're feeling, giving yourself permission to be honest about your fears and desires. These moments can be as simple as noticing your breath when anxiety rises, or allowing yourself to cry without pushing the feelings away. The goal here isn't to "fix" everything immediately but to create a steady thread of empathy and care for your inner world.

Contrary to what many believe, reconnecting with yourself means more than mindfulness or self-awareness; it means rebuilding trust. Loss or betrayal shakes your foundational sense of trust—not only in others but in your own judgment and worth. When your heart has been broken, you might find yourself second-guessing your choices, doubting your intuition, or feeling unworthy of love or kindness. These feelings are common and understandable, but they don't define your future. Reconnection invites you to look beneath these doubts and rediscover the parts of you that are resilient, kind, and capable.

On a practical level, this might look like carving out time each day for solitude, meditation, or journaling—anything that allows you to hear your own voice amid the external chaos. It's about creating a sanctuary inside your life, a place where your true self can emerge without fear of judgment. This sacred inner space becomes the soil where new growth can begin, rooted in acceptance rather than judgement.

Reaching out to others plays an equally important role in this healing process. It might feel risky at first, especially if previous relationships ended in pain or betrayal. But human connection is a powerful antidote to despair when approached with authenticity and care. It's important to recognize that not every relationship will be a source of healing—and that's okay. Reconnection means being intentional about who you allow into your life, setting boundaries that protect your well-being, and seeking relationships that offer mutual respect and compassion.

Sometimes, reconnecting with others means leaning into communities that offer you understanding and support. This could be close friends, family members who truly listen, or even support groups where you feel seen and heard. Vulnerability might be scary, but it's often the bridge that carries us from loneliness to belonging. When you allow yourself to be vulnerable in a safe space, you create room for empathy, shared healing, and sometimes even new beginnings.

It's equally vital to remember that reconnecting with others requires patience and balance. You don't have to rush into new connections or immediately repair damaged relationships. Sometimes the best act of self-love is to wait and honor your own readiness. Other times, it means having honest conversations about your needs and limits. Both approaches create a foundation where new connections can be genuine and nurturing rather than a source of renewed pain.

There's also a profound power in forgiving yourself and others during this stage. Forgiveness doesn't erase the hurt or forget what happened. Instead, it frees you from the weight of anger and resentment that can keep you stuck in the past. By forgiving—even in small ways—you clear space inside your heart for trust and love to grow again. This is a gift you give yourself first, an act of courage that reinforces your worthiness of peace and happiness.

Another essential aspect of reconnecting involves reclaiming your own story. When trauma shakes our world, it can feel like the story of who we are has been rewritten by pain. But you have the power to retell that story, honoring every chapter—the joyful moments, the heartbreak, the resilience, the lessons learned. As you reconnect with yourself, you allow your true narrative to emerge, one that acknowledges the pain but also celebrates your strength and capacity for growth.

One practical tool to support reconnection is the practice of presence with others and yourself. Being truly present—whether listening to a friend or sitting with your own thoughts—anchors you in the moment, grounding your experience rather than letting your mind spiral into past regrets or future anxieties. It's a way to rebuild trust with your own feelings and with those who hold space for you. This attentive presence creates a sacred environment where healing can genuinely unfold.

It's also important to honor the rhythms of your healing. Some days, reconnecting will feel possible and natural. Other days, it might seem like a monumental task. This ebb and flow is part of the process and learning to ride these waves with compassion means being gentle with yourself and others. There's no "right" pace—only your pace. Trust that each small step matters and accumulates into meaningful progress.

Reconnection is, in many ways, an invitation. It's an invitation to show up for yourself and others with openness despite the risk of pain. To reclaim your capacity to love, trust, and be trusted. To remember that beneath every ending lies the possibility of new beginnings. Healing gathers us back to a place where vulnerability becomes strength, and where love—most importantly, self-love—becomes the cornerstone of living fully again.

As you practice reconnecting, allow yourself to celebrate even the smallest victories. Maybe today you reached out to a friend, or today you spoke kindly to yourself instead of with blame. Maybe you sat quietly and listened to how you really felt. These moments are not insignificant; they are the steady bricks building the foundation of your renewed life. Healing isn't about perfection—it's about presence, courage, and compassion. With every connection you nurture, whether inward or outward, you reclaim pieces of your heart and rebuild a life that feels whole again.

Learning to Trust Again

When trust shatters, it feels like a fundamental part of your world has crumbled. Trust is the invisible thread that connects us to others and ourselves—it's what lets us open up, lean in, and believe that people and life won't let us down at every turn. After experiencing betrayal, loss, or heartbreak, that thread can seem irreparably broken. But learning to trust again doesn't mean rushing back into the way things were before. It's about rebuilding that thread one careful stitch at a time, starting from deep within.

The journey to regain trust is never linear, and it certainly isn't easy. The emotional walls you've built are there for a reason—they're your protection, your armor against more pain. While these defenses can feel like a safe fortress at first, they often isolate you from the very connections that bring meaning and healing. The paradox is that trusting again calls for courage to be vulnerable despite knowing how much it hurts when vulnerability is met with harm.

Trusting again begins first with trusting yourself. This step is often overlooked because it seems simpler to fixate on trusting others. But self-trust is the foundation on which all other forms of trust rest. It's believing in your own judgment, intuition, and strength to navigate life's uncertainties. Maybe you got burned before because you ignored your gut or stayed silent when something felt off. These experiences can turn that internal compass into a battered relic, leaving you doubting every decision. Yet rebuilding self-trust means honoring your feelings and experiences without judgment, respecting your limits, and recommitting to honoring your truth—no matter how small the step.

Think of self-trust as a muscle; it weakens with neglect but strengthens with repeated use. Start by making small promises to yourself and keeping them—whether that means setting aside time for your well-being or acknowledging your emotional needs without shame. Every time you show up for yourself, you reinforce the belief that you're reliable and worthy of care. It's not about perfection but consistency. This growing confidence arms you against the noise of self-doubt and the sting of past betrayals.

Once you've begun to reestablish trust within, reaching out to trust others becomes less daunting. But it's important to realize that trusting again is not about handing over your whole heart all at once. It's about allowing yourself to let someone in—just a little at a time. Vulnerability doesn't mean throwing caution to the wind; rather, it's a gentle unfolding. You might start with small acts of openness, sharing a thought, or asking for support. Notice how people respond—do they respect your boundaries, listen without judgment, and show up consistently? These little moments build a mosaic of trust, piece by piece.

Many people find themselves stuck, waiting for another person to prove they're trustworthy before risking connection again. But what can help is to see trust not as an all-or-nothing guarantee but as a willingness to risk, coupled with healthy boundaries. Trust is inherently a risk because it always holds the possibility of disappointment. Recognizing and accepting this complexity can bring freedom, shifting the focus away from trying to control outcomes to simply choosing to engage with openness when it feels safe enough. Sometimes, the safest choice is to wait longer, and that's okay. There's no timeline for rebuilding trust.

It's also crucial to be aware of the red flags and not ignore your intuition. Learning to trust doesn't mean ignoring potential warning signs or ignoring how someone's actions make you feel. Healthy trust balances hope with caution. What feels safe for you might be different from someone else's threshold, so honoring your unique limits is part of this process.

The experience of betrayal often leaves you questioning not just others but the world itself. You might wonder if love is worth it or if relationships are just a setup for pain. These doubts are valid and need compassionate attention. Trusting again is also about coming back to the fundamental truth that life, while unpredictable, is not inherently unsafe. This shift requires reconnecting to the present moment—which means tuning in to what is here now instead of habitual fears of what might happen. Sometimes, the mind will try to protect you by playing worst-case scenarios on repeat. Learning to notice this pattern and grounding yourself in what you can control right now is a powerful trust-building tool.

Another part of learning to trust again involves forgiving—not necessarily excusing past hurts, but releasing the grip bitterness and anger can hold on your heart. Forgiveness is a decision to let go of carrying the heavy burden of resentment which only weighs you down further. It's a gift you give yourself more than the other person. When you can forgive, you create space to rebuild trust, starting with yourself and hopefully radiating outward.

Trust is not static; like courage, it requires practice and repetition. There will be moments when fear creeps back in or when old wounds feel fresh again. That's natural, and it doesn't mean failure. Healing trust means learning to sit with discomfort in a new way, recognizing it as part of growth rather than a signal to retreat. With every conscious choice to engage rather than withdraw, you build resilience that can withstand future challenges.

Sometimes, it helps to lean on community during this process. Surrounding yourself with people who have demonstrated kindness and reliability offers a living example of what trust can look like. These connections remind you what it feels like to be seen, valued, and supported without pretense. They serve as a mirror, helping repair the shattered reflection of trust inside. Whether it's friends, family, or support groups, these positive relationships are balm for the wounded heart.

Patience is another essential ingredient. You might find yourself wanting to move quickly—maybe because you miss the feeling of connection or crave reassurance—but rushing trust only invites setbacks. Time doesn't heal all wounds by itself, but time paired with compassionate effort and intentional steps does. Every choice to open yourself a little more, affirm your worth, and surround yourself with respect and care nurtures trust's slow revival.

Rebuilding trust also means redefining what it means for you going forward. You might carry the scars of your past, but those scars don't have to dictate the script of your future. Trust can look different now—it can be wiser, more discerning, and still alive. Trusting again is about holding space for imperfection, both in yourself and others. It's releasing unrealistic expectations and choosing connection, even when it's scary or uncertain. It's a brave stance, a dance between heart and mind, vulnerability and boundaries.

In the end, learning to trust again is an act of hope. It says, despite pain and loss, you believe in the possibility of love, safety, and joy. It's a gentle but fierce affirmation that your heart still knows how to open, even after being broken. Rebuilding trust means reclaiming your place in a world where you can be seen, heard, and loved—not because you're flawless, but simply because you are.

Releasing Fear and Opening Up to Life

Fear is one of the most stubborn barriers standing between us and the life we long to live after emotional wounds. When heartbreak, betrayal, or loss shakes the foundation of our world, fear often sneaks in quietly—fear of getting hurt again, fear of being vulnerable, fear of stepping into the unknown. It's natural. Fear is a protective mechanism, designed to warn us about potential threats. But when it stays stuck in overdrive, it traps us in a cage of isolation and keeps us from truly embracing life's possibilities.

Releasing fear isn't about ignoring it or pretending it doesn't exist. It starts by acknowledging it with kindness. You don't have to battle that fear alone or view it as a sign of weakness. Instead, imagine sitting with it just long enough to understand what it's really trying to tell you. Is it the fear of rejection? Or the fear of being abandoned once more? Sometimes fear simply points to deeper wounds that haven't fully healed. Recognizing the origin gives you the power to shift your relationship with that fear from one of enemy to one of guide.

Opening up to life again means reclaiming your courage to feel deeply—even when what lies ahead is uncertain. Courage doesn't mean rushing headfirst recklessly. It means a quiet, steady willingness to let your heart be vulnerable, even when it's fragile. It means allowing yourself to hope again despite past hurts. And yes, that's incredibly hard, especially if you've faced emotional storms that left you feeling broken. But it's essential. Because life truly begins when we stop hiding behind walls and start moving toward connection, even if the path is messy and imperfect.

Fear has a way of making us believe we must protect ourselves at all costs by shutting down, numbing out, or pushing others away. But ironically, these defense mechanisms often keep us locked inside the very pain we want to escape. One moment, you might feel isolated in your grief, convinced that nobody else really understands what you're going through. The next, you might catch yourself building walls, thinking that letting anyone in is too risky. Here's the truth: healing asks for the opposite. It invites you to gently lower those barriers, bit by bit, when you're ready, not to rush the process but to gradually rediscover the safety in openness.

Part of releasing fear involves retraining how you talk to yourself internally. The mind has a habit of spinning worst-case scenarios or clinging to the echoes of past betrayals. But your thoughts aren't facts; they're simply stories you tell yourself. By catching those stories and softly challenging them, you create space for more compassionate and balanced perspectives. Instead of falling into "I'm broken" or "I'll never be okay," you can start shifting toward "I am healing" and "I am learning to trust again." This internal shift reframes fear from something paralyzing into a memory of pain that no longer controls your present.

Sometimes, opening up to life requires external gestures— like reconnecting with old friends, seeking new experiences, or even letting yourself feel joy in unexpected ways. Fear whispers that these things will only lead to more hurt, but healing reveals a different truth: joy and connection don't erase the pain; instead, they exist alongside it, reminding you that life's richness still pulses within you. When you allow yourself little moments of happiness—even if it feels fragile at first—you're planting seeds for bigger blooms of hope and love.

Cultivating a sense of safety within yourself is also vital. This doesn't mean the world suddenly becomes without risks, but it does mean you develop a sanctuary inside, a place you can return to where you feel grounded no matter what external storms rage outside. This space is built with routines, self-care, and boundaries that honor your healing journey. The more secure you feel inside, the greater your capacity to approach new relationships and opportunities without the heavy weight of fear. You might notice that you can listen to your needs more clearly and respond with gentleness instead of harsh judgment.

Another powerful way to release fear is through presence—grounding yourself in the moment rather than letting your mind spiral into "what ifs" and imagined heartbreaks. When your attention turns to the here and now, fear's grip often loosens. You begin to notice the small details: the warmth of sunlight on your skin, the sound of birds, the way your breath flows. This shift helps remind you that you're alive, you're still here, and the future remains unwritten. It also opens the door to wonder, curiosity, and the basic human capacity to find meaning even in pain.

Opening up to life also means recognizing that vulnerability isn't synonymous with weakness. In fact, it's one of the greatest strengths we possess. When you let yourself be vulnerable, you give others a chance to see the real you—scarred, healing, and human. This openness can invite connection, empathy, and even love back into your life. It's a risk, yes, but the kind of risk that brings a life worth living, richer and fuller than before.

It can help to remind yourself that no journey toward healing is linear. There will be days when fear creeps back in, when you feel like retreating into yourself again. That's normal. Healing isn't about perfection but progress. Every time you face fear—whether by reaching out, by speaking your truth, or simply by choosing to keep going—you reinforce your bravery and resilience. It becomes a muscle that grows stronger the more you use it.

Letting go of fear also often involves forgiving yourself for past choices or the harsh ways you might have judged your own emotions. Maybe you've blamed yourself for things beyond your control, or felt weak for being knocked down by heartbreak. Releasing that inner burden clears space not only for peace but also for life's next chapter. When the weight of fear and self-reproach lifts, you can breathe deeper and see the horizon with clearer eyes.

Ultimately, releasing fear and opening up to life is a radical act of self-love. It says, "I am worthy of healing. I deserve joy. My heart still has room for love." It's about stepping out—even if a bit shakily—into the vastness of possibility that lies ahead.

The journey ahead isn't about forgetting the pain; it's about living in spite of it, drawing strength from the cracks where light now shines through.

In this process, don't underestimate the power of small, consistent choices. Each time you invite a new experience, each moment you give yourself permission to feel hope, you rewrite the narrative of your story. Over time, fear becomes less of a dictator and more of a faint whisper you acknowledge but no longer obey. Life, in all its unpredictable beauty, waits patiently for you to open your hands and heart again.

From Surviving to Living

There's a subtle but profound shift that happens when we move from merely surviving to actually living again. Surviving is about getting through the day, often by sheer force of will, clutching tightly to whatever scraps of strength remain. It's that raw, unfiltered existence where the main goal is to endure pain, silence the chaos inside, and keep breathing. But living—real living—is something different. It's about reawakening a sense of possibility, hope, and connection to life beyond the wounds. It asks us to step out of the shadow of hurt and into the light of growth, even if our steps are small and uncertain at first.

After emotional trauma, surviving can feel like an achievement in itself. It's a testament to your resilience that you're here reading these words, still willing to try. But the truth is, survival is only the starting point. When we linger there too long, we risk getting stuck in a limbo of pain and numbness, unable to rediscover the color and warmth that once filled our world. Living, on the other hand, invites us to reclaim not only our days but our spirits. It means choosing curiosity over fear, hope over despair, and presence over avoidance.

Shifting from surviving to living isn't an overnight transformation. It's more like learning to walk again after your heart has been broken. At first, every movement feels shaky, awkward, and uncertain. There are moments when you might stumble or fall back into old patterns—those safety nets of survival—that seem easier because they're familiar. Yet, with practice, patience, and gentle self-encouragement, you can start to move forward with a little more confidence and grace.

One of the most important truths to hold onto in this phase is that living doesn't mean forgetting what happened or pretending the pain never existed. Instead, living means integrating the experience—the heartbreak, the loss, the betrayal—into the narrative of your life without letting it define you completely. You honor the story by recognizing its impact while also opening space for new stories to flourish. This is where hope takes root: when you allow your heart to hold both the sorrow and the possibility of joy.

It's also vital to remember that embracing life again often means redefining what living looks like for you personally. Society might paint a picture of what a 'happy life' or 'recovery' should look like, but your journey is your own. It could mean rediscovering passions, cultivating new relationships, pursuing goals that once seemed impossible, or simply learning to savor the small moments of peace and beauty that pepper each day.

There's no prescription or checklist here—just an invitation to show up for yourself in ways that feel authentic and nurturing.

At times, moving forward might feel overwhelming. The world may seem harsher, brighter, or simply different than before. It's okay to feel fragile and uncertain; this transition calls for kindness, especially toward yourself. When you catch yourself questioning your worth or doubting your path, gently remind yourself that growth is rarely linear. There might be setbacks and days when survival feels like the only option, and that's okay too. Healing is more like a winding trail than a straight highway.

Some moments will surprise you, though. You might catch yourself laughing unexpectedly, craving connection, or feeling a curious spark about the future. These are signs that your heart is softening and opening, that you're preparing to step beyond survival and into a fuller experience of living. Pay attention to these gentle invitations—they're guideposts pointing toward renewal.

Learning to live again often requires a new relationship with your own emotions. In survival mode, feelings can feel like threats—dangerous storms to be weathered or avoided. Living asks you to lean into your emotional life with curiosity and courage, not as a victim but as a witness. This doesn't mean forcing yourself into premature optimism or toxic positivity. It means allowing your feelings to be what they are, understanding them, and then choosing to move forward in spite of them.

Another key part of moving from surviving to living rests on reconnecting with your body. Trauma and heartbreak don't just inhabit our minds—they echo through our muscles, breath, and posture. When you allow yourself to move, to breathe deeply, to rest fully, it sends a message to your nervous system that you're safe enough to feel alive again. Simple practices—stretching, walking outdoors, or even dancing in your living room—can kindle a spark of vitality that logic alone can't ignite.

Yet, living fully also means reclaiming your boundaries and your sense of safety in the world. When trust has been broken, it's natural to guard yourself closely, to protect the fragile heart within. But the life you want to build beyond survival includes learning to recognize and honor your limits while gently expanding them over time. This balance fosters trust—both in yourself and in the world around you. It's through this practice that you create a space where joy and love can once again find a home.

Spirituality, whatever it means to you, can be a powerful anchor in this passage. There might be times when you look to something greater than yourself for solace or guidance—a quiet prayer, meditation, or simply a sense of awe at the world's beauty. These moments can remind you that even in the midst of pain, life is vast, mysterious, and endlessly capable of surprise. They help shift your perspective from one of scarcity to one of abundance—a necessary step to transform survival into living.

Remember, living doesn't require perfection. It asks for presence, practice, and the willingness to keep moving ahead, even on days when your heart feels heavy or broken. Celebrate every small victory: a day without crying, opening up to a friend, setting a boundary, or simply getting out of bed. These are more than just acts of endurance—they are signs of you reclaiming your life bit by bit.

So how do you know when you've truly moved from surviving to living? You begin to notice moments when your heart feels spacious—not empty or overwhelmed, but open and ready. You find yourself dreaming about new possibilities or caring deeply for yourself and others once again. Your pain, while still present, becomes part of the landscape rather than the entire view. And most importantly, you feel increasingly empowered to choose life, with all its messiness and beauty, rather than just withstand it.

This journey isn't about racing to a finish line or proving something to anyone. It's about honoring your story, honoring your heart, and gently stepping into a life that feels worth living. If you can hold that intention, no matter how far away it seems now, you're already on your way beyond survival—to a life rich with meaning, love, and true peace.

Reclaiming Joy, Purpose, and Wholeness

After enduring the storm of heartbreak, loss, or betrayal, reclaiming joy might seem like a distant dream, almost impossible to reach. But it is not only possible—it's essential. Joy isn't about forcing a smile or pretending pain doesn't exist; it's about finding those moments that light you up again, however small and fleeting they may feel at first. This process is about tuning back into your own capacity for happiness, however it manifests, and allowing yourself to experience it without guilt or hesitation. Joy, purpose, and wholeness are like seeds waiting to be nurtured in the soil of your healing.

The first step in reclaiming joy is recognizing that your capacity for happiness hasn't vanished just because you're hurting. It might be buried beneath layers of grief and fear, but it's still there. Sometimes, joy shows up in the quietest ways—like soaking in sunlight, hearing your favorite song, or sharing a meaningful conversation. It's those tiny moments that remind you there is more beyond the pain, something worth holding on to. Embracing these sparks isn't trivial; it's a radical act of self-care and hope.

Purpose enters the picture when you begin to feel ready to look beyond survival. It doesn't have to come as a grand, life-altering mission overnight. Sometimes, purpose is as simple as waking up each day with the intention to heal, to reconnect, or to contribute to others' well-being. This sense of meaning provides a foundation, helping to steady your heart when waves of doubt or sorrow roll in. Purpose breathes a new kind of energy into your days—it's a beacon that guides you out of the fog of pain.

Wholeness might feel like the hardest thing to reclaim after emotional wounds because it suggests going back to a state of being complete and well—something your broken heart refuses to believe is possible right now. But wholeness isn't about perfection or pretending you are unharmed. It's about integrating your pain as part of your story, making peace with what's happened, and realizing that healing is a messy, non-linear journey. Wholeness means accepting every piece of yourself, including the parts that hurt, and seeing that they don't define you but instead shape the resilient person you're becoming.

It's critical to understand that reclaiming joy, purpose, and wholeness is not a destination but a continual practice. Some days you'll feel vibrant and alive, and others you'll feel hollow and tired. Both states are valid, and each has something to teach you. Allowing yourself to live through these emotional cycles without judgment creates the space where true transformation can unfold. Over time, these moments accumulate, stitching together a renewed sense of self that is stronger and more compassionate.

Finding joy again also involves shedding the heavy cloak of shame and blame that often follows emotional trauma. If you lost trust in yourself or others, it's natural to feel fractured and wary. But the weight of self-recrimination keeps you locked in pain. The path to joy asks you to start disentangling from that grip, replacing shame with curiosity about yourself and your experience. Understanding that your feelings are valid and your reactions human allows healing light to seep into those darkened corners.

Purging yourself of burdensome guilt or anger can be a crucial part of this reclamation process. It doesn't mean forgetting what happened or excusing those who hurt you, but rather choosing to stop letting those emotions dominate your internal world. Imagine clearing space in a room cluttered with heavy furniture—you don't take away the room's history, but you make room for fresh air and light. In the same way, freeing your heart from toxic attachments allows you to invite hope, joy, and renewed purpose.

Building rituals that honor your emerging joy and purpose can provide a steady rhythm to this work. These are personalized acts—small or significant—that connect you to what matters. It might be journaling your feelings and dreams, spending time in nature, practicing gratitude, or celebrating your daily wins no matter how small. Rituals become sacred moments that remind you your life is still unfolding, even after immense heartbreak. They anchor you to the present and cultivate resilience from within.

It's important to reach out and reconnect with both yourself and others as part of reclaiming wholeness. Connection isn't about rushing into new relationships or forcing yourself to "get over" the past. Instead, it's about rebuilding trust first within your own heart—the confidence that you can be safe and loved. When you nurture self-trust, the world becomes less intimidating. You'll find yourself ready to slowly open up to others again, knowing that vulnerability, while scary, can lead to richer, more authentic bonds.

Along this journey, embracing your uniqueness is a powerful act. Trauma often comes with feelings of fragmentation or invisibility. Yet, your individual pain and healing are what make you who you are. Reclaiming joy and purpose means stepping into your own light without comparing your path to others. Healing doesn't have a timeline or a single blueprint; it's as unique as your fingerprint. Trust your instincts, honor your pace, and celebrate the progress, however subtle it may seem.

Wholeness, in this sense, is the integration of your experiences into a coherent narrative that supports your growth rather than detracts from your worth. This means allowing yourself to be both wounded and brave. To feel loss deeply and to still believe in love and possibility. It means holding your heart with tenderness, even in its broken places, and recognizing that those places can also hold seeds of strength and wisdom.

This reclamation invites a shift in perspective—moving from seeing yourself as a victim of circumstance to the author of your own story. It's a gradual reawakening of agency and creativity. You get to decide who you become beyond the hurt. Even on days when hope feels thin, there's power in the choice to reach for it. Each step toward joy, purpose, and wholeness is a statement: I am here. I am still growing. I am worthy of a full, vibrant life.

Sometimes, life's heartbreaks reshape us into someone we might not recognize at first. That's okay. The new you is not less than who you were; it's a version forged in endurance and courage. Reclaiming joy and wholeness means honoring not just what was lost but what you're rediscovering and becoming. It's the promise that even when your heart feels shattered, it still beats with infinite potential.

In the quiet moments of your healing, remember this is your sacred work. There is no shame in needing time, in falling back at times, or in asking for help. Joy and purpose aren't just emotions; they're the lifeblood that can carry you through to the next chapter. When you make space for them, you reclaim the wholeness that's been waiting inside you all along—the wholeness that affirms: you are not broken beyond repair. You are whole and capable of love again.

CHAPTER 4

MOVING FORWARD WITH PEACE

Stepping into a life where peace is possible doesn't mean forgetting the hurt or pretending everything's fine; it means choosing to carry your story with gentle strength and using what you've learned to shape a future that honors your resilience. This stage calls for embracing every fragment of your journey—pain included—as a source of wisdom rather than a weight to bear alone. It's about building a daily practice of self-kindness, leaning into moments of calm, and trusting that healing isn't linear but profoundly transformative when you allow yourself the grace to move at your own pace. Here, peace isn't a distant goal but a quiet presence that grows each time you forgive, each time you show up for yourself, and each time you turn your scars into stepping stones toward a brighter, more empowered tomorrow.

Writing a New Chapter

There comes a moment on the path of healing when the weight of what's been lost, broken, or betrayed begins to ease just enough to imagine something new—something whole— waiting on the other side. This moment is like standing at the edge of a blank page, notebook in hand, ready to write your own story again. It's not about pretending pain never happened or rushing past the sorrow you've carried. Instead, it's about acknowledging your resilience and the quiet strength that has grown from the cracks. Writing a new chapter means choosing to live with intention, crafting a life that reflects who you are becoming rather than what you've endured.

Starting this chapter doesn't require grand gestures or dramatic reinventions. Sometimes, the smallest acts—the gentle shift in your morning routine, a new phrase you whisper to yourself when doubt creeps in—are what begin to reshape your world. Think of this chapter as a garden you plant seed by seed. Some days, the soil feels fertile and ready; other days, the ground seems stubborn and unyielding. But with patience, compassion, and care, what seemed barren slowly returns to life. The new chapter is not a quick fix; it's an unfolding, delicate process that flows naturally when you allow yourself the grace to heal fully and authentically.

One of the hardest parts is coming face-to-face with the fact that you have to let go of the old story you've been living— the narrative that might have defined you through pain, loss, or betrayal. That chapter served a purpose; it spoke to your survival instincts and your capacity to endure. But if you cling to it too tightly, you risk being trapped in a loop where your identity becomes a reflection of suffering rather than growth. Writing a new chapter means stepping away from the shadow of what happened and leaning into the light of what's possible. It's a bold act of reclaiming your voice, your dreams, and the kind of peace you crave.

You might find that writing this new chapter involves rewriting some of your beliefs about yourself and the world around you. Maybe the story you've told yourself includes lines like "I'm broken," "I'm not enough," or "I don't deserve happiness." These lines, as harsh as they sound, are only drafts, not destiny. In creating new pages, you get to challenge these assumptions, to replace them with affirmations that honor your worth and your capacity for joy. This is where healing and hope entwine, where self-compassion becomes the pen guiding your narrative forward.

Imagine for a moment how it feels to look back at your life from the vantage point of this new chapter. Will you see a story of defeat or a tale of courage? Will your pages be stained with regret and bitterness, or will you find inked promises of renewal, kindness, and gratitude? The beauty of writing a new chapter is that it's yours in every sense of the word—full of possibility, empathy, and a genuine intention to move forward with peace. You may stumble. You may pause and turn back. But the pen is still in your hand.

Sometimes the hardest part is deciding where to begin. The good news is that there is no perfect starting point. Healing doesn't follow a clear timeline, nor does it conform to any set pattern. Your new chapter might start with a conversation you hesitated to have or with setting a boundary you thought impossible. It might come in the form of nurturing a hobby that brings you peace or reaching out for support when loneliness threatens to overwhelm you. Each choice, no matter how small, builds momentum toward a fuller life—not defined by the heartbreak but enhanced by the wisdom it offered.

It's important to acknowledge that writing a new chapter is not about erasing the past but integrating it in a way that empowers you. Your experiences, no matter how painful, have shaped the person you are becoming. When you embrace the full spectrum of your journey, you create a narrative rich with depth and honesty. This kind of storytelling fosters healing because it doesn't sidestep truth; instead, it holds it gently and allows space for growth alongside grief.

Think of this new chapter as a story of courage measured not by the absence of scars but by the willingness to carry those scars with grace. It's about walking forward without shame or fear, knowing that your history is a foundation, not a cage. Your heart can hold the past and still make room for joy, connection, and hope. In doing so, you teach yourself the most important lesson of all—that healing is an ongoing act of bravery and love.

At times, you may feel uncertain about what this new chapter should look like, and that's natural. Writing a story without a clear plot or roadmap can feel overwhelming. But remember, life rarely unfolds in straight lines. Embrace the twists and turns, the pauses and surprises. These are the elements of an authentic journey. The beauty here is in your willingness to show up for yourself again and again, even when the way forward isn't clear. The act of writing your new chapter—of choosing to keep going—becomes its own kind of healing.

One of the most transformative parts of creating this fresh start is learning to trust yourself. After heartbreak or betrayal, that trust can feel fragile. You might question your judgement, your worthiness, your ability to love again. But trust doesn't have to be all or nothing—it grows in moments of gentle care and honest reflection. As you write this new chapter, remind yourself that your feelings are valid, your boundaries are important, and your needs deserve respect. In this space, trust has room to bloom, nourishing your soul and guiding your steps toward peace.

Writing a new chapter also invites the power of choice back into your life. It reminds you that although you can't rewrite the past, you get to decide how you live today and tomorrow. This realization ripples outward, influencing how you engage with others and how you nurture relationships. You find yourself drawn to people and experiences that support your well-being and step away from those that drain or diminish you. The chapter you're writing becomes a testament to your growth—a declaration that peace and joy are worth pursuing, even in the wake of heartache.

The truth is, you're far more than the sum of your wounds. Writing a new chapter means recognizing the inherent value you bring to the world simply by being yourself. It's about celebrating the light within you—the parts of you that have persisted through stormy seas and are ready now to shine brighter. This part of your journey might be quiet and subtle or bold and dynamic, but it is always profound. When you commit to this new chapter, you are saying yes to yourself in the most powerful way possible.

So, as you stand at the edge of this new beginning, take a deep breath and allow yourself to feel both the weight and the wonder of what's ahead. Writing a new chapter is an act of courage, a step toward peace that honors everything that's come before but refuses to be held captive by it. You hold the pen; now, let the story unfold in whichever way feels true to you. The pages are blank, the possibilities endless, and your heart ready to heal and grow once more.

You Are Not What Happened to You

When life's storms shake the ground beneath your feet, it's easy to believe that the disaster defines you. The heaviness of loss, the sting of betrayal, or the sharp ache of a breakup can feel like permanent labels stamped on your soul. But here's the truth you need to hold close: you are not what happened to you. What happened may have shaped part of your story, but it does not dictate your identity or your worth. You are so much more than the pain you've endured.

This distinction matters because when we confuse our experiences with who we are, it's like carrying chains forged from our suffering. They weigh us down, stifle our growth, and dim the light inside us. Your pain is undeniably real, and it's a part of your journey, but it is not your essence. Your core remains intact, waiting to be nurtured back to life with kindness and understanding.

Many people who've walked through heartbreak or trauma find themselves trapped in a loop of self-judgment. They say things like, "I'm broken," or "I'm damaged beyond repair." These thoughts are not only untrue, but they are also dangerously limiting. When you think this way, you're viewing yourself through a cracked mirror—distorted and incomplete. Healing begins when you learn to see yourself through a clearer lens, one that reflects compassion and the possibility of renewal.

It takes courage to separate who you are from what you have suffered. This isn't about minimizing your pain or pretending it didn't happen; it's about refusing to let that pain define you. Imagine your life as a book. The chapters of heartbreak and loss are significant, but the pages ahead remain blank, waiting for new stories filled with hope, strength, and growth. The past doesn't have the power to erase the person you are becoming.

Real transformation is about reclaiming your narrative and realizing that your identity is not anchored in trauma but in resilience. You have endured, you have survived—and that alone is a testimony to the strength in your spirit. You can choose to wear your scars as marks of experience rather than wounds of shame. They remind you how far you've come, not how far you've fallen.

It's important to recognize the role of self-talk in this process. The stories you rehearse in your mind shape your reality more than any external event. When you catch yourself saying, "This is who I am now," ask if that's truly the whole truth. Chances are, it's a version of you filtered through pain, not through possibility. Challenge those assumptions gently. Give yourself permission to dream of a self that is healing, hopeful, and whole.

Another key part of this journey involves separating your emotions from your identity. Feeling sad, angry, or betrayed does not make you weak or flawed. Those feelings are your mind and body's natural response to loss. They are signs that you are human—not symptoms of some brokenness that defines your very being. When you allow yourself to experience these emotions without labeling yourself as broken, you open the door to deeper healing.

For many, this process also includes forgiving themselves for the perceived mistakes made during painful times. The harsh inner critic that chastises you for "allowing" hurt or "not seeing it coming" needs to be quieted. Your intentions were always to protect yourself and love deeply, even if the outcome was painful. Self-forgiveness is an act of reclaiming your dignity and refusing to let the past diminish your value.

In practical terms, what does it look like to stop defining yourself by what happened? It can begin with small shifts—a gentle reminder each morning that today is a new opportunity to cultivate peace within. When old memories or feelings surface, acknowledge them, but don't invite them to take over your sense of self. Replace "I am broken" with "I am healing." Instead of "I am unloveable," say "I am worthy of love." These affirmations may feel awkward at first, but repeated over time, they help rewrite your inner script.

It's also helpful to remember that your experiences, no matter how painful, don't make you weak; rather, they reveal your humanity. Everyone carries wounds—some are visible, some hidden beneath layers of protective armor. What sets the healing soul apart is not an absence of pain, but a willingness to face it and refuse to be defined by it. This strength is quiet but fierce, gentle but unyielding.

When you accept that you are not a prisoner of your past, you reclaim your power. The power to choose how you move forward, to write the next chapters, and to create meaning from the chaos. This is the essence of moving forward with peace. It's a conscious decision to stop fighting against the things you cannot change and instead focus on nourishing the person you are still becoming.

Letting go of the notion that your past dictates your identity also frees you from the heavy burden of shame and guilt. Shame shouts that you are inherently flawed, while guilt can trap you in cycles of regret. But clean separation between your actions or what happened and your worth allows you to feel those emotions without being swallowed by them. You start to see them as experiences that teach, rather than character flaws that define.

This is a profound shift—one that often takes time and patience. It's natural to feel tied to your pain, especially in early stages of healing. The mind wants to make sense of chaos by categorizing you in a limited way. But healing invites you to expand your view. You are a complex being with immense capacity for love, growth, and renewal—not a simple summary of your worst moments.

Inside you lies a reservoir of strength. Sometimes, it's hidden under layers of hurt and fear, but it's there. Accessing it means turning your gaze inward with kindness instead of judgment. It means committing to seeing all parts of yourself—both the wounded and the whole person—and honoring both as vital to your journey.

In time, you will discover that your story of pain can be transformed into a story of courage. When you remember you are not what happened to you, you open the door to self-compassion, possibility, and peace. This revelation is the foundation for moving forward—not by erasing your past, but by learning to live beyond it with grace and strength.

So, as you continue this journey, remember this simple truth: your identity is yours alone. It cannot be stolen by heartbreak, betrayal, or loss. Healing begins the moment you claim that truth and let go of the illusion that your worth depends on your history of pain. Embrace the person you are becoming, and step forward with the quiet confidence that you are more than your scars—you are an enduring spirit capable of love, growth, and peace.

Your Healing Toolbox

Healing is never a one-size-fits-all journey. Each person's experience with emotional pain is unique, and the tools that help one individual may differ from another. That's why having a well-rounded healing toolbox is essential—because it offers a variety of options to lean on when the weight of heartbreak, loss, or betrayal feels too heavy to bear.

Think of this toolbox as a collection of practices, techniques, and mindsets that you can reach for whenever you find yourself stuck in the quicksand of emotional turmoil. These aren't unrealistic quick fixes or empty promises. Instead, they are grounded approaches that foster resilience, self-compassion, and gradual recovery. It's about building a foundation from which peace can grow, bit by bit.

Everyone's healing journey involves layers—sometimes you're ready for deep introspection, while other times you may just need a simple act of self-kindness to get through the day. That's the beauty of your healing toolbox: flexibility. It adapts to your needs in the moment.

Mindfulness is crucial in this toolkit. It's easy to get swept away by the chaos inside your mind—the spinning thoughts, the relentless "what ifs," and the echo of painful memories. Mindfulness teaches you to gently observe these experiences without judgment, creating a small but significant space between your suffering and your awareness of it. In other words, it helps you realize that while you can't always control what happens to you, you can control how you relate to it.

Practicing mindfulness can be as simple as focusing on your breath for a few minutes or noticing the sensations in your body without trying to change them. These moments of presence might seem small, but they build emotional muscle over time. You start to see your feelings as passing visitors rather than permanent residents.

Another powerful tool is **journaling**. Writing down your thoughts and feelings might feel awkward at first, especially if you haven't been in the habit of expressing your inner life on paper. But journaling can unlock clarity, release emotions you weren't even fully aware of, and give you a space where your pain is valid and heard without interruption.

Don't worry about grammar, spelling, or coherence. This isn't a performance; it's raw, honest communication with yourself. Sometimes, pouring out your story in black and white can reveal patterns, shifts, and small victories that you might miss otherwise. Your journal becomes a sacred container—it's private, judgment-free, and entirely yours.

Therapy is another cornerstone in the healing toolbox. It's not a sign of weakness; it's a courageous act of self-investment. A skilled therapist provides safe, compassionate support that helps you untangle complicated emotions, understand destructive patterns, and develop healthier coping strategies. They serve as a guide, helping you navigate the rough terrain when you feel lost and overwhelmed.

There are many therapeutic approaches—whether it's talk therapy, cognitive-behavioral techniques, somatic therapy, or trauma-informed counseling—and finding the right fit is part of the journey. If starting therapy feels intimidating, consider that it's okay to try a few therapists before settling on someone who truly resonates with you.

Your healing toolbox also benefits from a regular **spiritual practice**, whatever that looks like for you. You don't have to adopt a religion or follow a specific doctrine; spirituality can be grounded in connecting with nature, practicing gratitude, or cultivating a personal sense of meaning and wonder.

Spirituality offers a reminder that you are connected to something larger than your current pain. It's about nurturing a sense of hope when things feel hopeless and embracing a faith in the possibility of growth beyond suffering. Even simple acts like lighting a candle, meditating in silence, or listening to music that stirs your soul can deepen this inner connection.

Beyond these foundational tools, the healing toolbox should include **self-care practices** tailored to your needs. This might be as ordinary as setting boundaries to protect your energy, spending time doing activities that bring you joy, getting enough rest, or nourishing your body with wholesome foods. These acts aren't indulgent—they're essential.

When emotional pain is raw, it's tempting to push yourself through or distract with busyness, but true healing often requires a gentler approach. Self-care isn't about perfection or achieving constant productivity—it's about honoring your limits and recognizing when to pause and replenish.

Sometimes, emotions like anger or grief can feel like wild storms inside you. It's okay to let them express themselves, and healthy outlets for these feelings form another important tool. Creative expression—through art, music, movement, or writing—can provide a release that words alone often can't. These allow your pain to transform rather than being trapped or ignored.

At the same time, your toolbox includes practical **routines and rituals** that anchor you. These might be morning moments of quiet intention, a nightly practice of gratitude, or simply consistent sleep schedules. Rituals bring rhythm and stability when everything else feels unpredictable. They build a container within which healing can take root and flourish.

One tool many overlook is learning to cultivate **community and connection**. Healing was never meant to happen in isolation. Pain can be isolating, but leaning on trusted friends, support groups, or loved ones creates a living network of compassion and understanding. You don't have to carry your burden alone, and allowing others in (even in small ways) can remind you that you are valued and supported.

It's important to remember that sometimes, the toolbox may feel empty or the tools feel out of reach. That's a natural part of healing. The work is often non-linear, with days that feel hopeful followed by setbacks. That's okay. Having even a small set of tools handy means you've got options, even if you have to nibble on progress slowly.

Every item in your healing toolbox builds upon another. Mindfulness supports journaling by increasing self-awareness. Therapy can help you develop better self-care habits. Spiritual practice can sustain your emotional resilience when grief feels unbearable. When used together, these tools become a powerful web of support.

Ultimately, your healing toolbox is about empowering you to become the healer of your own heart. You don't need someone else to fix you, nor do you have to erase the pain overnight. What matters is that you gather your tools, learn how to use them gently and consistently, and give yourself the grace to heal in your own time and way.

In moments of despair, remember: peace isn't something you find outside—it's something you cultivate from within. Your healing toolbox is the bridge that connects the fractured pieces of your heart to a future where wholeness, joy, and love can live again.

Mindfulness, Journaling, Therapy, and Spiritual Practice

As you navigate the delicate path toward peace after emotional upheaval, grounding yourself through mindful awareness can be a powerful ally. Mindfulness invites you to gently anchor your attention to the present moment, without judgment or the urge to change what is. It doesn't mean ignoring pain or rushing toward false positivity; instead, it offers a way to hold your suffering with tenderness, making space for it to soften and transform. When your heart feels shattered, moments of mindful breathing or simple sensory awareness can act as a lifeline, pulling you back from overwhelming waves of distress and into a steadier place of calm.

This practice, though seemingly simple, has profound implications. It cultivates a new relationship with your inner world, one that replaces resistance with acceptance. You might notice how emotions arise and pass, like clouds drifting across a wide sky, and slowly begin to recognize that you are the sky, not the storm itself. Mindfulness builds resilience, helping you break free from the repetitive loops of rumination or self-criticism that often hold emotional pain hostage. Even just a few minutes a day can chart a remarkable shift in how you experience pain and healing.

Journaling serves as another heartfelt companion on this journey. The act of putting pen to paper unlocks a unique kind of clarity—feelings that seem tangled in your mind find their way out, shaped into words that carry meaning. Writing without censorship or editing allows your rawest emotions to be witnessed by yourself, which can feel enormously validating when you've been carrying invisible grief. It's in these pages that you might find unexpected insights, uncover hidden layers of your experience, and hear your own voice become an advocate rather than an accuser.

Journaling doesn't demand perfection or literary skill; it simply asks you to show up honestly. Sometimes, the pages become a safe cage to shout into when the world feels too harsh. Other times, they cradle your most tender hopes and dreams for the future, coaching you gently toward new possibilities. Over time, this practice transforms into a mirror reflecting not just where you've been in pain, but also where you're headed in healing.

Alongside mindfulness and journaling, engaging with therapy can bring profound pockets of relief and understanding no one else can offer quite the same way. Therapy creates a space for you to safely explore your emotions with someone trained to listen deeply without judgment. When you're weighed down by betrayal, loss, or heartbreak, it's easy to feel isolated, as if no one could truly grasp your suffering. But in therapy, you can uncover the roots of your pain, dismantle harmful stories you tell yourself, and learn new ways to cope that don't involve numbing or avoidance.

A skilled therapist also acts like a guide who helps you make sense of the chaos inside, untangling the knots that have formed over time. By naming these patterns and reframing experiences through a compassionate lens, therapy enables you to reclaim your narrative. It's not an instant fix, and that's okay. Healing runs on its own timetable, but having someone walk with you through the process eases the burden and reminds you that you are not alone.

Spiritual practices, whatever form they take, offer another dimension of support. Whether through prayer, meditation, connection with nature, or engagement with a faith community, spiritual work taps into something greater than yourself. This connection can be a profound source of comfort and meaning when everything in your life feels unstable or unfair. The spiritual path often invites surrender—not as giving up, but as letting go of the need to control every outcome and trusting that healing unfolds in divine timing.

Many find that spiritual practices also cultivate a deeper sense of belonging—not just to a higher power, but to the larger web of life. This can alleviate feelings of isolation and remind you that your suffering, as unique as it feels, is part of a shared human experience. Rituals, whether large or small, hold space for remembrance and renewal, marking transitions from pain toward peace. Light a candle, sit in quiet contemplation, or repeat a mantra—these acts can anchor you when the world feels unsteady.

Integrating these four tools—mindfulness, journaling, therapy, and spiritual practice—doesn't have to be complicated or overwhelming. You might start with one and let the others evolve naturally as your healing unfolds. The key is to approach them with compassion and patience, knowing that progress is not linear and that setbacks are part of the process. Often, it's in the small, consistent daily choices to show up for yourself in these ways that true transformation takes root.

There's something profoundly empowering about building your own healing toolbox. These practices are yours to shape, to use whenever you need to steady yourself, to listen deeply, and to nurture your heart back to life. They become trusted friends who remind you that peace is not a destination but a practice—and that you are capable of creating pockets of calm even in the most turbulent times.

Remember, healing isn't about forgetting or minimizing your pain. It's about learning to live with your story in a way that honors where you've been while opening to where you want to go. Mindfulness, journaling, therapy, and spiritual practice each guide you back to yourself, helping you reclaim your power, your voice, and ultimately, your peace.

Becoming the Healer of Your Own Heart

Healing doesn't come from some magical external source—it begins with you. No one else can mend your heart the way you can; that's the quiet power of becoming your own healer. When you face heartbreak, loss, or betrayal, it can feel like the world has stripped you of your strength. But in truth, the process of healing is about reclaiming that strength, piece by piece, moment by moment.

It starts with acknowledging that your pain is real and valid. Too often, we rush to silence our wounds, pretending everything's fine because it's easier than confronting vulnerability. But when you lean into the discomfort instead, you open the door to transformation. Healing requires courage—the bravery to face the raw, messy parts of yourself and your experience without shame or judgment.

One of the hardest, yet most liberating steps is choosing to take responsibility for your healing journey. This doesn't mean blaming yourself for what happened. It means deciding that you won't stay a victim of circumstances or other people's actions. You become the steward of your own recovery, nurturing your heart back to health with tenderness and patience. This shift releases you from a cycle of helplessness and regret, instead planting your feet firmly on the ground of self-empowerment.

Being your own healer doesn't imply going it alone either. It's a reminder that within yourself, you hold the authority to decide what support you need and when to seek it. Surrounding yourself with trusted friends, guides, or professionals can complement your inner work. But at the center of this process is your own willingness to show up for yourself every day—the quiet choices to listen, soothe, and believe in your capacity to grow.

There's no fixed timeline for healing. Some days might feel like steps forward; others might feel like setbacks. That's all part of the process. The heart isn't a race to a finish line but a journey that asks for steady curiosity and sometimes fierce compassion. Becoming your own healer means developing a new relationship with time itself—trusting that healing unfolds in its own rhythm, often in unexpected ways.

A key part of this transformation is learning how to nurture your heart with kindness. In the wake of trauma or loss, it's natural for self-criticism and doubt to creep in. You might catch yourself replaying harsh judgments or questioning your worth. Replacing those narratives with affirming and gentle self-talk rewires how you relate to yourself. Imagine speaking to yourself like you would to a dear friend who's hurting— patient, understanding, and full of hope. That practice can change everything.

Another powerful tool in becoming the healer of your own heart is honoring your emotional truth. This means resisting the urge to bury feelings or rush to fix pain. Instead, you invite your emotions to be seen and felt—not as enemies to be conquered but as signals that guide you toward deeper self-awareness. Through this lens, grief, anger, sadness, and confusion aren't weaknesses; they're part of the language your heart uses to process its experience.

In this process, boundaries become essential. Protecting your energy, saying no when you need to, and creating safe spaces for yourself are acts of healing in their own right. When your heart has been broken, it's easy to accept less than you deserve or to overextend yourself in attempts to regain control. Setting clear limits helps rebuild trust with yourself and creates the conditions for genuine recovery.

Becoming your own healer also means learning how to tune into your needs and honor them without apology. This might be resting when exhaustion settles deep in your bones or choosing activities that bring a spark of joy even if it feels fleeting. The small acts of caring for yourself—whether it's making a nourishing meal, going for a walk, or simply breathing deeply—accumulate over time to rebuild a foundation of safety and wellbeing.

At times, you'll encounter resistance—old fears, doubts, or beliefs that encourage you to stay stuck in pain. It's important to recognize these as part of the healing dialogue, not permanent barriers. What once protected you might now hold you back. Becoming your own healer involves gently challenging these parts of yourself, learning to listen without giving them control, and gradually expanding your capacity for hope and trust in the future.

The journey may call you to reinvent how you see your story. Instead of defining yourself by the heartbreak or betrayal you experienced, you begin to see yourself as a survivor, a learner, a warrior. This shift doesn't erase the pain but integrates it into your identity in a way that empowers rather than diminishes. It's about holding your story with both tenderness and strength, acknowledging the wounds while also claiming the wisdom they've offered.

Part of becoming a healer involves embracing the simple yet profound practice of presence. When the heart feels shattered, the mind often races ahead—dodging grief or anxiously trying to fix things. Learning to be present with whatever arises, without rushing or escaping, creates a sacred space within you. This space becomes a refuge where healing can quietly take root and grow.

This path is deeply personal. What heals one person may look different for another. Your way of becoming the healer of your own heart will be shaped by your unique history, needs, and desires. The common thread is the commitment to yourself—deciding every day, through your actions and intentions, that your heart's peace matters and is worth fighting for.

Remember, the act of healing itself is a radical declaration: that pain will not have the final word. Each step you take toward caring for your wounded heart writes a new chapter— one of resilience, hope, and ultimately, love. You carry within you everything required to reclaim your joy and your peace. Becoming the healer of your own heart is the bravest, most loving gift you can ever give yourself.

Turning Pain into Power and Wounds into Wisdom

When life leaves us battered and broken, the natural instinct is often to hide from the pain, to push it down so deep that it no longer surfaces. Yet, pain is not just a dark shadow to be escaped; it can become the very forge where strength and insight are shaped. This transformation doesn't happen overnight. It asks for courage—the kind of courage that comes from facing your deepest wounds honestly and gently, turning what once hurt you into the foundation of new power.

At its core, turning pain into power means reclaiming your narrative. Instead of letting your story be defined by loss, betrayal, or heartbreak, you become the author of your own healing journey. You gain the ability to see your suffering not as a mark of weakness but as a badge of resilience, a testament to having walked through the fire and still choosing to stand. This shift in perspective doesn't deny the pain or erase it; rather, it honors it as a vital part of becoming more whole.

It's important to recognize that wounds, especially emotional ones, are also teachers. They bring lessons—sometimes harsh, sometimes illuminating—that might have stayed hidden if it weren't for the fracture. In learning to listen to these lessons, you develop wisdom. This kind of wisdom isn't about having all the answers. Instead, it's about cultivating a relationship with yourself where curiosity and compassion replace judgment and shame.

For many, this process starts with vulnerability—the willingness to lean into discomfort and uncertainty. To move from pain to power, you must first get comfortable with sitting in your emotions without trying to fix or escape them immediately. Being present with your hurt allows you to see the parts of yourself that need care and attention. Each tear, every ache holds a hidden message, often pointing toward what's been neglected or needs change.

That's why this phase of healing is as much about presence as it is about progress. You don't rush through the pain or pretend it's less than it is. Instead, you gently explore it, giving yourself permission to grieve, rage, or feel lost. This honest encounter creates space for growth because it affirms that your feelings matter—and that you matter. Wounds, after all, need to be witnessed before they can truly begin to heal.

The power that emerges from this intimate attention to your pain is transformative. When you start accepting your scars, you begin to see them as part of your unique story rather than flaws that diminish your worth. This acceptance fosters an inner strength that doesn't depend on external validation. It's a raw, authentic power rooted in knowing that you've survived what you thought you couldn't—and in knowing you're still here.

Turning wounds into wisdom also means reframing what it means to be "broken." Society often tells us we must be perfect or whole to be valuable, but real wholeness includes imperfection. It embraces the cracks because they let in light. These cracks, or wounds, are inside all of us, and acknowledging them connects us to a more authentic, compassionate sense of self. It also deepens our empathy for others, building bridges instead of walls.

Another key element in this transition is harnessing the lessons your pain is giving you to make intentional choices moving forward. For example, your heartbreak might teach you about boundaries you didn't have before, or a betrayal might reveal your own patterns of trust and vulnerability. Each experience sharpens your awareness and equips you to protect your heart better without closing it off altogether.

This process is never linear. Some days, your wounds feel fresh and raw; other days, you recognize how far you've come. Both states are valid and necessary. Healing doesn't mean forgetting or moving on as if nothing happened—it means integrating your experiences into your life story in a way that empowers you, not diminishes you.

Power born out of pain often becomes a quiet strength rather than a loud declaration. It's the steady, grounded energy that carries you through difficult moments, the inner voice reminding you that you are capable of weathering storms. This power also inspires hope. Even in darkness, a spark remains—a reminder that life is still unfolding, with possibilities waiting to be embraced.

Wisdom gained from wounds invites you to approach future challenges differently. You develop a deeper trust in your intuition, a more compassionate inner dialogue, and a greater awareness of what truly nourishes your soul. This intuitive wisdom guides your decisions, relationships, and self-care practices in ways that align with your healing journey.

What's beautiful about turning pain into power is that it changes not just how you see yourself but how you connect with the world. You might find yourself drawn to help others who suffer or become more patient with the struggles of those around you. Your own journey equips you with empathy and insight, creating a ripple effect that transforms not only your life but also the lives you touch.

Still, it's essential to remember that this transformation requires patience and kindness toward yourself. You won't always get it right, and setbacks are part of the terrain. But with each step—however small—you're moving out of victimhood and into authoring your own healing. The power you gain is not about control over external circumstances; rather, it grows from reclaiming your inner landscape and making peace with your past.

In this way, wounds become wisdom not by erasing the scars but by learning how to live fully and bravely with them. You become someone who walks forward with peace—a peace not born from avoidance, but from the fierce, tender courage of having been broken and choosing to rise anyway.

So as you continue to move forward, hold onto this truth: your pain has purpose. It's shaping you into a wiser, stronger version of yourself—one who understands the depths of suffering and the heights of healing. The chapter you write from here will be one of empowerment, built upon the foundation of every wound you've endured.

Turning pain into power and wounds into wisdom isn't about denying the darkness you've faced; it's about using that darkness to reveal your own light. This light shines quietly, steadily—guiding you through the night until you reach a place where peace doesn't just feel like a distant dream, but a living, breathing reality.

CONCLUSION

Healing a broken heart isn't about forgetting or pretending the pain never happened. Instead, it's about learning to live with the memories, the scars, and the lessons in a way that no longer holds you captive. This journey is tough because it asks you to face your deepest vulnerabilities head-on and to cultivate compassion for yourself when it feels like all your strength has been drained. It's a process that unfolds slowly, sometimes imperceptibly, but every step, no matter how small, is a victory in reclaiming your life.

Each person's path toward peace looks different, shaped by their unique experiences and emotions. What matters most is that this journey honors your pace and your feelings without judgment. There's no "right" way to grieve or move on, and there's no finish line where pain suddenly evaporates. Instead, healing is more about integrating your suffering into your story so it becomes a wellspring of resilience and wisdom rather than a weight that drags you down.

It's natural to want quick fixes or immediate relief, but that's rarely how true healing unfolds. Instead, it asks you to slow down, turn inward, and meet your own pain with courage. You learn not to shut down, but to open up to your emotions, allowing yourself the full spectrum from sorrow to hope. This openness doesn't make you weak — it makes you profoundly human and, eventually, deeply free.

The chapters before this one have taken you through the raw edges of heartbreak, the tangled thickets of self-doubt, and the gradual rebuilding of trust and joy. Now, as you stand at this crossroads, it's important to realize that peace is not the absence of pain but the ability to live fully despite it. This is a radical kind of peace — one that embraces both shadow and light, holding your past, present, and future with equal gentleness.

Many who have walked this path find that their losses, while devastating, become sources of unexpected growth. The cracks in your heart are exactly where the light can shine through. The pain reshapes you, yes, but it doesn't define the rest of your life. There's a richness that emerges when you let go of the need for control and perfection, when you accept that healing is messy, nonlinear, and unpredictable.

It's okay to feel afraid as you take these next steps. Fear is part of the process, signaling that you're moving beyond old comfort zones into the unknown. But within that unknown lies the possibility of rediscovering yourself, your passions, and your capacity to love — not only others but yourself. This kind of self-love is the foundation for lasting peace; it's what anchors you when life feels uncertain.

As you continue on this journey, remember that healing is also about connection. Finding or creating safe spaces where you can express yourself without shame is crucial. Whether through friendships, communities, or quiet moments alone, these spaces are where you cultivate strength and authenticity. They remind you that your story matters and that you are never truly alone, no matter how isolated heartbreak might make you feel.

There will be days when the weight of grief feels unbearable and others when joy peeks through unexpectedly, like sunlight breaking through a storm. Both are part of the rhythm of healing. Celebrate small victories — a moment of laughter, a peaceful night's sleep, a day free from overwhelming sadness — because these are the seeds of hope growing beneath the surface. Over time, these moments accumulate, building a new sense of wholeness.

Healing also means reclaiming your power. While you can't change what happened, you can choose how you respond to it. This book encourages you to turn pain into power by learning from your wounds rather than being defined by them. That doesn't mean you erase your hurt or avoid memories; instead, you integrate them, allowing your past to inform your wisdom while refusing to imprison you.

This journey requires patience and kindness toward yourself. It's tempting to rush through the pain or to push it away entirely, but true peace demands presence. When you sit with your feelings — even the difficult ones — you build emotional resilience. You learn that heartache is not a permanent residence but a transient storm that passes, revealing clearer skies.

Moving forward doesn't mean you forget. It means you carry your story with grace and choose what it will mean to you. It means embracing uncertainty with faith in your ability to navigate life's challenges with strength and compassion. You are far more than your heartbreak; your soul remains intact and capable of deep love, joy, and connection.

In the end, this healing journey is an act of courage and self-respect. By facing your pain, you show up for yourself in a way that affirms your worth beyond any loss. You become your own healer, your own refuge. With every breath, every step, you move closer to a life where peace is not the absence of trouble but the presence of hope.

Let this be your truth: Finding peace when your heart is in pieces is not only possible but within reach. The road may twist and wind, but it also leads to rediscovery, renewal, and ultimately, a profound freedom few ever imagined. Embrace the journey — for it is yours and no one else's — and trust that on the other side of pain lies not just survival but a thriving, radiant life waiting to unfold.

APPENDIX

As this journey draws to a close, this appendix is here to be your quiet companion—a place to return to whenever you need a gentle reminder that healing is possible, even when it feels impossible. Sometimes the most powerful support isn't found in lengthy explanations or complex theories, but in simple tools, words, and practices that you can carry with you day after day.

Within these pages, you'll find a collection of reflections, exercises, and practical suggestions designed to meet you exactly where you are. They're meant to help you pause, reflect, and reconnect with the parts of yourself that might feel buried beneath the pain. There's no right or wrong way to use these; take what you need, leave the rest, and come back when your heart calls for it.

Healing isn't linear. Some days will feel lighter, and others heavier. That's okay. This space honors that complexity and holds room for all your feelings without judgment. It's here to remind you that while the heart can shatter, it also has an incredible capacity to piece itself back together, often stronger and more resilient than before.

In this appendix, you won't find step-by-step commandments for "fixing" your heart, but rather invitations— soft nudges toward self-care, self-understanding, and gentle courage. These are the small acts that stitch up wounds over time: a morning breath, a kind word to yourself, a moment of stillness amidst the chaos.

Remember, this is your journey. There's no deadline, no finish line except the one you set. Whenever you feel lost or overwhelmed, return here to find solace, encouragement, and the quiet wisdom that lives within you. Your heart may be in pieces today—but with patience, grace, and time, those pieces have the potential to create a mosaic more beautiful than you ever imagined.